Conor Woodman is an economist, author and presenter. His first book *Around the World in 80 Trades: The Adventure Capitalist* and the accompanying four-part television series for Channel 4 tell the story of how he left his job in the City, sold his London flat and embarked on a round-the-world trading adventure. Travelling through four continents in five months, he turned his hand to making a profit out of everything from camels in Sudan to inflatable surfboards in Mexico, to discover how real people make real money in real markets. Visit his website at www.conorwoodman.com

Praise for *Unfair Trade*

'Many books denounce rapacious Western corporations, but few combine – as Woodman's does – first-hand global reportage with practical advice on change. From Congo to China, and from chocolate to cotton, he seeks commerce with a conscience'   *Independent*

'Conor Woodman takes the dismal out of the dismal science. He's written an alternative travel guide to the global economy'   Liam Halligan, *Sunday Telegraph*

CONOR WOODMAN

Unfair Trade

The shocking truth behind 'ethical' business

BUSINESS
BOOKS

Published by Random House Business Books 2012

4 6 8 10 9 7 5

Copyright © Conor Woodman 2011

First published in Great Britain in 2011 by Random House Business Books
Random House, 20 Vauxhall Bridge Road,
Lonon SW1V 2SA

www.randomhouse.co.uk

Addresses for companies within The Random House Group Limited can be
found at: www.randomhouse.co.uk/offices.htm

The Random House Group Limited Reg. No. 954009

A CIP catalogue record for this book is available from the British Library

ISBN 9781847940704

Penguin Random House is committed to a sustainable future for
our business, our readers and our planet. This book is made from
Forest Stewardship Council® certified paper.

Printed and bound in Great Britain by Clays Ltd, Elcograf S.p.A.

Contents

Acknowledgements

First and foremost I'd like to thank everyone who appears in the text of the book. It would not have been possible to tell this story without the openness and honesty of the people in it. I was constantly amazed and often humbled at the willingness of individuals in extraordinarily desperate circumstances to talk to a complete stranger about the details of their lives.

There are also several people who do not appear in the book whom I need to thank. A book like this cannot be researched without considerable logistical support, which depends on contacts and recommendations from people who have been there before you. I will be eternally grateful to all those that helped me visit far-flung corners of the world safely. In particular, I would like to thank Carlos Coffin and Eric Pickles for their assistance in penetrating the world of the Miskito divers in Nicaragua, Kevin Sites and Amani Matabaro for enabling me to get into and out of the Congo in one piece, Lianne Gutcher and James Brabazon for letting me peek at their little black books in Afghanistan, and Kate Lazarus, Jill Xiaohua, Kim Taylor and everyone at Global Witness for their support on the Asian leg of the book.

I am also indebted to my publisher at Random House, Nigel Wilcockson, for his insightful and sympathetic edits, my agent

Gordon Wise for his unwavering support, and my parents Ciaran and Miriam Woodman for all their ideas and suggestions during the drafting of the book.

And to Victoria Shalet – thank you for your endless patience and support, for listening time and again, and for always being the first face I saw after every trip.

Introduction

This book is about the poor. Specifically, the working poor in the developing world. The people who do jobs that you probably wouldn't like to do for a wage you probably wouldn't be able to live on. These people are the farmers, the miners, the fishermen and the factory workers who often produce the goods that eventually end up in your shopping basket. Those products get there thanks to any number of big businesses: the big restaurant chains, the big electronics companies, the big drug companies, the big car companies . . . the list goes on and on and on. This book is about how those people are affected by those companies and therefore, because it's our shopping baskets we're talking about, it's also about how they are affected by you and me.

You may, like me, have wondered before why it is that our favourite brands import billions of dollars' worth of goods from the developing world and yet the people who produce them are still so badly off. Why can't the big businesses, from whom we buy our food, our gadgets, our clothes and all that other stuff, do more to ensure that the people who farm it, fish it, assemble it or mine it work in safe conditions or get paid a sufficient sum to ensure that they aren't forced to live their lives on the edge of existence?

If you have wondered about these things, then the chances are you're one of the millions of people who are starting to be a bit more selective about the goods they buy. There has been a rapid increase in the past ten years in 'ethical awareness' on the high street. Sales in ethical and environmental products are increasing exponentially year on year, which suggests that even more people are asking questions about where their purchases are coming from, from whom they have been sourced or how they have been produced.

We are now in a position where we can express our personal ethical values through our choice of coffee or chocolate or bananas or phones or a whole range of other products, and we may well make decisions prompted by a logo or message on packaging that effectively tells us that we're doing the right thing. More and more goods these days carry the logos of ethical labelling organisations like Fairtrade Foundation, Rainforest Alliance, Forest Stewardship Council and UTZ CERTIFIED. That logo or message, then, is a very powerful marketing tool. In fact, it's big business in itself. The Co-op's Ethical Consumer report puts the total value of ethical products in our shopping baskets at over £36 billion in 2009 and estimates that the total value of Fairtrade-labelled products alone will top the £1 billion mark in the UK in 2011. Despite the recent economic downturn, sales of ethical products in the UK have actually increased by 20 per cent in the last two years. But is there a danger that the marketing edge the ethical business label gives companies becomes the driving force, rather than the desire to make a positive difference?

A couple of years ago, I was sitting on a train, watching the countryside go by, sipping a cup of coffee. I glanced down briefly and happened to notice that the coffee cup had a picture of an African farmer on it and a message: 'By drinking this coffee you are enhancing the lives of the villagers of Busamanga, Uganda.' Next to the message was a logo for the ethical labelling organisation Fairtrade Foundation, with their tagline: 'Guarantees a better deal for Third World producers.'

As a concerned consumer who wants to help poor farmers in African villages, this is exactly the kind of label that I'm meant to look out for. I should have been reassured by it and felt better that I had made an ethically conscious purchase. But I slowly became aware of a nagging doubt. It just didn't sit easily with me. I found myself thinking about some awkward questions. Am I really enhancing these farmers' lives? Are they really getting a better deal? Is it even possible to improve people's lives by buying a certain type of coffee? I thought again about the logo and wondered whether '*Trying* to get a better deal for Third World producers' might be more accurate. It also occurred to me that the fact that something was being done made me feel better about myself. A second later, I questioned whether making me feel better about myself was quite the intention of the scheme when it was set up.

Turn on the TV or browse the Internet and you can hardly avoid coming into direct contact with the reality of what life is like for a vast number of poor people in poor countries around the world. The media has given us a stronger connection to what is happening in developing countries, but while events of major political or economic significance are covered exhaustively, we rarely hear the day-to-day stories of the ordinary people who work in the fields or down the mines or out on the fishing boats. How can we ever keep up with what is going on in their lives or the lives of our farmers in Africa unless we actually go there to see for ourselves?

Six months after that train journey I was in Cameroon writing a piece for a popular travel magazine. For a few days I holed up in a modest hotel along the shore near the town of Limbe. At lunchtime the menu in the hotel kitchen generally offered guests a simple choice between chicken and fish. Since I was so close to the coast, I usually chose the fish because I was confident that what was on my plate would be wonderfully fresh.

From my window every morning I could see a local guy called Patrice fishing off the shore from his pirogue. Patrice would always fish in the shallower waters within a mile or two of the black sand beach. I would see him silhouetted against the morning sky casting out his line hoping that he'd pull in a nice tuna or a snapper for the chef to serve up that lunchtime. Sometimes, further out in the deeper water, a large trawler would pass along the horizon, dwarfing Patrice's little boat as it scooped up fish by the thousand.

When evening falls in Limbe, the market square in the centre of town is the place to go to sit and enjoy a beer or something to eat. One evening, while I was out walking, I dropped in and spotted Patrice eating with his family. On seeing me, Patrice insisted that I come over and join them; right away I noticed that, although they too were eating fish and rice, the bones on their plates looked very different from those of the big snapper that I'd eaten a few hours earlier.

Patrice explained that the trawlers I'd seen from the shore were Chinese-owned. In exchange for Chinese investment in various construction projects within Cameroon, the government had signed away wholesale fishing rights in all their deep water to Chinese fishing companies. The result is that local fishermen can now only line fish in the shallow waters close by, and this brings in nowhere near enough fish to feed their families, let alone the wider population. So the rare snappers that Patrice can catch are extremely valuable and he sells them to tourists like me who can afford them, while the locals can only afford to eat dried fish imported across the desert from Morocco.

This is, of course, shocking. Any fair and reasonable person would say it is wrong. Yet global trade is full of these kinds of anomalies. How can we reconcile ourselves to a world where a cup of ethically branded coffee bought in a Western high street costs about the same as a fish supper for a tourist in Cameroon, and that both remain far beyond the means of those who produced them in the first place?

This book is in part the result of the shock that I felt on that trip to Cameroon. I realised that it's easy to take an ethical standpoint from afar, so I decided to try instead to witness things at first hand – to do this, I had to make a series of journeys. I wanted to see how my early views stood up when exposed to the reality of life in the developing world, which is occasionally nasty, often brutish and sometimes needlessly short.

The result has been a year spent in often uncomfortable circumstances, sometimes even dangerous ones. I have travelled from Latin America to the Far East to look at how ethical the companies are that put the food on your plate or the gadgets in your pocket. And I have travelled from Central Asia to Central Africa to consider the impact some of our consumer choices have on the poorest people who work in the most desperate of circumstances. Finally I returned to Africa to look at some of the newer ideas being employed by companies who are managing their supply chains in more socially responsible ways.

My first concern was to check to what extent ethical claims made by big business actually stack up. If a company says we do X, Y or Z, should we accept this at face value? To answer that, I chose to look at one strand of the international food chain, and follow the supply of lobsters back to the waters from where they were caught. Several of the world's biggest restaurant chains buy lobster in bulk from suppliers in Latin America. Many make bold claims about their own ethical credentials and give sums of money to conservation projects. Sometimes, though, as I discovered, the reality doesn't quite live up to the hype.

Of course, once you start losing confidence in what you've been told, everything starts to look suspect. I therefore turned my attention to the 'good guys' – the various bodies such as Rainforest Alliance and Fairtrade Foundation – who have played such a major role in increasing our awareness of the problems of international trade. They clearly mean well, but do or can they really deliver on their promises? And what happens when their message becomes part of a large corporation's way of doing business? When McDonald's says, 'We support the Rainforest Alliance', what does this actually mean? And when Cadbury announce they're 'going Fairtrade' to the world's media, can we automatically assume that it can only be good news?

The challenges for big business, if it is to save the world's poor, though, go considerably beyond the concerns that organisations such as Rainforest Alliance and Fairtrade Foundation seek to address. They touch every transaction in our globalised economy. So, having looked at one or two relatively straightforward supply chains, I set myself the task of looking at some highly complex ones, the sort that involve manufactured goods that may bear a familiar brand name with excellent ethical credentials but that are actually the result of a complex web of trading relationships with companies and countries a long way removed from our purchase in the West of a new mobile phone or laptop or car or any of a thousand other desirable goods. Modern systems of manu-facturing in our increasingly globalised economy mean that whole links in the supply chain can be outsourced to far-flung corners of the globe a long way away from the scrutiny of the Western consumer. We are often fooled into thinking that our commercial relationship is only with our favourite brands, but when they form another relationship with some faceless factory in the Third World they can draw us into an uncomfortable *ménage à trois*.

These days it is virtually impossible to consider such relationships without considering the economic powerhouse that is contemporary China. I therefore decided to spend some time there, finding out what our insatiable demand for consumer goods actually means for the anonymous Chinese factory workers who toil to produce them. And then I went back yet another stage in the production process, visiting the jungles of Northern Laos, which provide China with essential raw materials. Consumers in the West are now highly dependent on the sorts of deals that China has set up with its trading partners. What about the terms on which these deals are struck and the reality of what they mean for the citizens of the producing country?

For my final expeditions I decided to open things up even further. Double standards and moral compromise are bad enough when you're talking about trade with countries such as Nicaragua, China and Laos, which, whatever other failings they may have, are at least relatively stable. But questions of morality and fairness become much more acute when you're looking to trade with countries that are abusing human rights on an almost unimaginable scale – the Democratic Republic of Congo and Afghanistan, for example.

Until I actually visited Congo I had assumed that all decent nations were following the United Nations' call for trade with the country to be suspended. I wasn't quite sure what that would achieve for Congo's citizens, but I could at least see a certain logic in the stance of the international community, given that the conflict there has led directly to the deaths of over 10 million people over the past decade. Yet one visit to a Congolese cassiterite mine was enough to show just how hollow a UN expression of outrage can be. Cassiterite is not exactly a household word, but the tin that is extracted from it crops up in just about every household and office electronic product that you can think of. How does it get there, if we don't trade with Congo?

From all this it may sound as though I have ended my journey possibly a wiser but much more cynical person: a believer in ethical business who, when confronted by the facts, has come to the reluctant conclusion that claims to the ethical high ground rarely stand up and that in any struggle between morality and hard-edged business, there will only be one winner, and that it certainly won't be morality. But that's not the case, and, strangely enough, it was my visit to Afghanistan which confirmed a belief that had sustained me through all my travels: it is possible to involve yourself in international trade and make money and yet, morally speaking, be able to hold your head up high. And in fact, in virtually every country I visited, I came across astonishing people who could tell astonishing success stories. It's just that their stories are not the ones you tend to hear.

This book will, I hope, help to redress the balance. It is not meant to be an exhaustive look at how big business operates, but rather a collection of case studies that together give a flavour of what life is like for some of the poorest workers in the world. And while it may shake your current assumptions, it does show that there is a way forward. It just happens not to be the one that most big business currently claims to embrace.

1

To die for

Nicaragua: the Miskito coast

'Better to be a sailor. Live longer'

I'm already feeling a bit uneasy. The sail of the 30-foot-long skiff I'm sitting in is pulled tight to the wind, and the huge logo emblazoned across it reminds me that this stretch of the Nicaraguan coast is prey to hurricanes. After Hurricane Felix devastated the coast in 2007, the American Agency for International Development sent emergency materials – food, clothes, tents and a large tarpaulin marked 'USAID – From The American People'. Most of the tarpaulin ended up being used as sails for skiff boats like this one. But the real reason for my unease is that I have agreed to make a deep-water dive.

We're now about a mile from the Keys. One of the divers I've joined drops the anchor while the rest of us take in the sails and begin to unload three canoes into the water. This is a very well-rehearsed routine and in less than three minutes we're sitting in a canoe with six air tanks. Wally, who has agreed to dive with me, is strong and muscular with arms and legs as thick as the mast of his boat. His equipment consists of a mask and flippers, a small black triangular plastic plate complete with Velcro strap for attaching the air tank, and one other crucial item: a long metal spike with a hook on one end. I'm struck by how primitive everything seems. There are none of the usual dials and gauges a diver in the West would expect to see, no way of telling how deep you are or how much oxygen you have left. I'm a little more fortunate. I at least have a dive computer, which will allow me to know how deep we are as well as whether or not I need to do a safety stop to decompress on my way back to the surface. Other than that, I will use the same rudimentary equipment as Wally.

Even before we descend, I do not feel safe. Wally's son passes me a tank from the canoe that he has already attached to the triangular plate. He hurriedly indicates to me to tie it round my waist. It feels horribly insecure. As I turn myself in the water, he reaches down and turns my air valve. A working mouthpiece will allow a diver to draw air from it as you would normally draw breath on the surface. However, this one is faulty so that the air jets out freely from the tank. It still works but if it did this during a normal dive then my instinct would be to return to the surface and have it repaired or replaced. Wally simply shrugs and shows me that his is broken too, as if to say that I should just hurry up and get on with it. I am not happy. I am feeling more than a little unnerved.

Wally descends head first. He's not hanging around. I like to descend feet first, slowly and steadily so as to give myself time to equalise the pressure in my ears. This is crucial if I am to avoid damaging my eardrums, but Wally's having none of it. If I'm not going to lose him in the gloomy water then I have to hurry down. I turn around so that I'm facing head first towards the bottom and kick with my flippers to follow him. A quick glance at my computer shows that I am already 6 metres down when suddenly and without any warning my head is spun around and my mouthpiece is ripped violently from my mouth. My tank has come loose from the Velcro strap and is heading back to the surface without me. I am 6 metres below without any air. Despite the fact that I am a very experienced diver, I begin to panic. For the first time in nearly

15 years of recreational diving I have to make an emergency ascent. I remember to exhale steadily on my way up so as not to run out of air and, more importantly, so as not to have my lungs explode when I reach the surface.

Back at the surface I can see Wally's son fishing my tank out of the water. I am still attached to the triangular plate. Wally's head soon reappears and he swims over to me looking confused before he realises what has happened. He shouts at his son. I imagine (at least I hope) that he's telling him his Velcro-ing skills need some work. I clamber back up to the canoe, untie my plate, retie the strap and try again.

What follows is the most uncomfortable dive of my life. I descend head first again with Wally constantly threatening to disappear out of view. My ears hurt the whole time and I am paranoid about my tank taking a solo trip back to the surface again. Struggling to breathe the whole time as the mouthpiece spews air constantly into my mouth, I repeatedly check my computer to make sure that I don't go below 18 metres, the depth from where I can still safely make an emergency ascent if something goes wrong. Somehow I manage to watch Wally at work.

Eventually we settle at a depth of around 16 metres and Wally begins to move along the wall of the reef's edge. For someone who dives every day, he still seems rather ungainly in this environment. He frequently uses the coral to anchor himself against the current while he peeks into the cracks and crannies between the rocks. Finally he turns and gestures for me to come nearer. I catch my first glimpse of what we've come for. Poking out from underneath a shadowy outcrop of rock are two long antennae.

Wally places his metal spike flat on the surface of the sea floor and carefully slides it deeper into the hole. The creature seems to know that something is afoot and draws himself in deeper into his hole, but not far enough. At once Wally is under him and, with one deft tug, the hook comes back out with its end buried deep under the flesh of the creature's belly. It twists and turns helplessly on the hook until Wally lifts it off with his other hand and turns the implement round to lance it through the back of the head with the spiked end. With it now safely dead, Wally carefully breaks off the head and places the valuable meaty tail into the net bag that he has deftly slung over his other shoulder. Wally has caught a lobster.

I give Wally an 'OK' sign, which seems to mean nothing at all to him. Then I indicate to him that I am going back up. He nods as if to say, 'Fine. See you later.' I am actually beginning to get quite cold, diving as we are without wetsuits. I head back to the surface, doing a decompression stop on the way just to be doubly safe and to keep my dive computer happy.

I throw my tank back on to the canoe and swim alongside the boat, happy not to be where Wally is. Wally's son is carefully paddling along, watching the water intently. The man in the canoe is known here as the 'dory man' and his job is to track the diver by following his bubbles on the surface. This is a lot easier said than done and by the time Wally emerges on the surface 25 minutes later he is at least 100 metres from where his dory man thought he was. And this is a calm day.

Wally and the dory man paddle towards each other and Wally passes his tank up to his son. By my computer's reckoning, he's been under for almost 45 minutes. This would be a pretty standard recreational dive – 16 metres for 45 minutes. As long as you had done a decompression stop on the ascent and then rested up at the surface for an hour, you could safely do another dive to a similar depth the same day. And maybe with another two-hour rest, a final dive could be safely attempted that evening. In less time than it has just taken you to read that observation, Wally is under the water again, descending head first, tying on a fresh tank as he goes. This time he is down for nearly an hour.

Wally doesn't make a single decompression stop on any of his 11 ascents that day. A safety stop doesn't cost anything other than a couple of minutes of time. But no one has ever explained to Wally why it is important. No one has explained to Wally that diving 11 times in one day is not safe or how depth and air gauges would increase his chances of survival. He has a job, and he does it unquestioningly.

Back on shore there are plenty of reminders of the dangers the job entails. Puerto Cabezas, or Bilwi as it is known to the local population, is a port town built along the long white sandy Caribbean shoreline of Nicaragua. It's a pretty typical Caribbean town; colourfully painted single-storey houses with corrugated iron roofs and a dozen or so large whitewashed churches.

I wander along with my contact and translator in Nicaragua, John Rivera Hudson, a short skinny bald man wearing a yellow T-shirt so big for him that it hangs over his shorts like a dress. On the end of his nose he sports a pair of round wire-framed glasses and on his feet a pair of bright pink Crocs. 'They're my wife's. We're the same size.'

As we make our way up the paved road that leads into town we pass first one and then another young man walking with a pronounced limp. At the park in the centre of town a group of men sit along a low wall talking loudly and swigging beer from brown bottles – unremarkable but for the row of crutches leant against the wall next to them.

John recognises a man who approaches us in what looks like a child's go-kart. The man introduces himself as Clevus Thompson. Clevus's home-made wheelchair has three wheels attached to a wooden frame, and in the centre there is a long shaft with a handle that turns a chain connected to the rear wheels. Clevus, dressed in a Boston Red Sox T-shirt and a pair of black jeans that hangs loosely over his withered legs, leans against the handle while he explains to me how he has come to end up like this. 'This happened to me diving,' he tells me. 'Twelve years, I've been diving on the boats for lobster, then I got sick. Now I can't work, so I have to beg around. Someone gives me something; that's the only way I can survive.'

Clevus is living with the consequences of repeated deep diving. Among divers in the developed world, decompression stops are an integral part of diving safely. If I'm diving 100 feet below the surface, say, then the air that I'm breathing from the tank contains nitrogen and oxygen, which are both absorbed into the blood through my lungs. I use up the oxygen as I swim about and the nitrogen goes round my body and back to my lungs from where I breathe it out again with the carbon dioxide I've produced. Because I'm 100 feet below the surface I'm breathing these gases under enormous pressure. The problem is that the nitrogen takes a minute or two to work its way around my body and back to my lungs. If, like Clevus, I return to the surface with the nitrogen still in my blood, it will expand, causing little bubbles to form in my arteries. This in turn can cause an embolism, leading to what is known as decompression sickness or 'the bends'. It can cripple you. At its worst, it can kill you.

Clevus is one of over 4,000 young men in this situation, although one could say that he is one of the lucky ones: each year 50 men perish diving for lobsters. All are Miskitos, indigenous Native Americans who have inhabited this part of the coast for hundreds of years. When British pirates roved the seas around here 300 years ago, and Bilwi was known as Bragman's Bluff, they swiftly discovered that the Miskitos could be valuable friends and allies. A mutually beneficial trading relationship was established that lasted through the days of the American revolutionary wars and the slave trade. The Miskitos and the British concluded a formal Treaty of Friendship and Alliance in 1740 and close contact continued for the next 100 years. Testament to this is the prevalence in the region of English names. The first four Miskito kings were named Jeremy, Peter, Edward and George.

Long after the British went, the American corporate juggernaut United Fruit came here to do business with the Miskitos and made hundreds of millions, exporting bananas and timber from the region. But bananas are no longer a viable commercial crop here due to endemic diseases, and in May 2006 the government announced an emergency ten-year nationwide ban on cutting and exporting mahogany, cedar, pochote, pine, mangrove and ceiba. The ban was announced as the 'green lobby' in Nicaragua reacted to deforestation in the Miskito region. In the past 50 years, 6,000 square miles of forest has been lost to logging and agriculture. Lobster fishing seems, on the surface at least, a much better and more sustainable economic activity.

Some 40 kilometres from Bilwi are the Keys, and among them Wipling Key: half a dozen shacks built on stilts driven into the ocean floor. From a distance they look like a floating village of 12 'houses' hovering over a shallow reef in the middle of nowhere.

Inside one of the houses there are three hammocks, one reserved at night-time for Wally, and one each for his children, a boy and a girl both in their late teens. As well as these three there are two other women living here, one of whom, Dora, has a husband and a five-year-old boy. Then there are the five other men who are here to dive. They are all from the town of Dakira back on the mainland. Wipling and several other similar Keys are known collectively as the Miskito Keys and each big village on the shore has a working offshore settlement like this during the lobster season from September until May.

'My boy likes to come out here to learn about life as a man,' Dora tells me as she scales a piece of fish. Crouched down on the deck out front, she deftly aims the scales over the edge and into the sea below, attracting a small school of brightly coloured fish. 'But I still like better my house on the shore. There I can walk around and go to church.'

During the day the hammocks are in constant use: if you're not eating, you're having a lie down. The house is never silent but filled with the constant chatter of the Miskito language. Wally has recently sunk a couple of extra stilts into the reef so as to erect a kind of outhouse where he has a sawn-down drum in which a fire boils a bubbling, dark caustic-smelling cauldron filled with sea cucumbers being preserved for export to new customers from China. In the centre of the deck is an old 1970s Formica-covered fridge that acts as a centrepiece and kitchen table. Obviously there's no electricity so plugging it in isn't an option.

Wally has been living like this out here for the past three weeks. In the far corner of the house are a couple of very large blue plastic chiller-tanks, each full of ice and capable of keeping up to 500 pounds of lobster cool for a week. And in the opposite corner are over 100 scuba air tanks. Hanging in the centre of the room is a set of old grocer's scales. Wally rents air tanks out to the other men for around $2.50 per tank, which includes transport on his boat out to the reef. If they come back with lobster then Wally weighs it and buys it from them there and then for around $5 per pound depending on size and weight.

Each week a boat comes out from Bilwi owned by what Wally simply refers to as 'the Company'. They pick up all the lobster, deliver fresh ice and diesel for the compressor and drop off some other provisions such as rice, cigarettes and a little rum. Wally sells the lobster on to the Company for closer to $7 per pound. As the only man with the facility to chill and store lobster, Wally is essentially the boss of this Key and makes a 40 per cent mark-up from everyone as a result.

A few of the people out on the Keys also bring in lobster caught in traps. Wally says he will buy it all regardless of how it was caught; it all goes into the same big blue chiller emptied by the Company every week. I wonder which method brings in the most. Wally shakes his head. 'Not too many people using traps. If you want to make money from lobster then you have to dive for it.'

I wonder aloud whether people living on the Keys realise that using traps is much safer than diving and therefore worth any slight loss in income that might result from this more hit-and-miss approach. Wally explains that even if he wanted to move to traps he would need at least 50 of them to begin catching enough to make a living, and each trap would cost him between US$25 and $30. 'Too expensive.' He shakes his head and laughs at the suggestion. Despite his relatively high status among the lobster fishermen, he simply doesn't have the sort of spare cash to be able to make such an investment.

'The Company' that Wally sells to is one of seven lobster-processing companies in Bilwi who collect lobster from the boats. They then ship them north to big US restaurant chains like the Red Lobster Company owned by corporate giant Darden. Lobster is big business and commands a high price, but US companies are alive to the importance of corporate social responsibility (CSR). Darden's website, for example, proclaims: 'Darden owns and operates 1,800 restaurants that generate more than $7 billion in annual sales . . . Darden is recognized for a culture that rewards caring for and responding to people.' Such companies know that diving for lobster is dangerous, that the people involved may well be injured or killed, and many US companies importing lobster from Nicaragua consequently insist that they never knowingly buy lobster caught in this way. The problem is that one lobster looks pretty much the same as the next. They don't come with a sticker that tells you how they were caught – dived for or trapped – and by the time they're sitting in the bottom of Wally's big blue chiller you'll never tell which was which.

The Miskitos no longer have a hereditary king; their new leader, the Reverend Hector Williams, is known as the Wihta-Tara, or 'Great Judge'. The short stocky man with a pencil-thin moustache in a smart pair of grey slacks and a white cotton shirt (rather than crown and cape) offers me a warm greeting outside his home. Hearing that his visitor has come all the way from London, Hector beams a broad smile. 'The British were our first father,' he says. And then, with an equitable tilt of the head, 'The Americans were our second.'

On 13 April 2009 the elders of 386 Miskito communities across the region gathered to elect their leader. In total over 1,400 elders voted. The system is a very public vote where the three candidates sit on a stage at the front of the gathering and each elder casts his vote by standing in front of his preferred man. Over half of those present lined up to support Hector Williams and his first act as their leader was to pronounce their independence from Daniel Ortega's Sandinista government in Managua.

With potential control of the taxes generated from Miskito resources, Hector was in no doubt about what he would address as a priority: 'We need hospitals and doctors and nurses of course, but first the people are hungry. That is first.'

It amazes me that these people can go hungry when they inhabit one of the most bountiful shorelines on earth. What about all the fish and lobster? 'The people do not afford to eat lobster. That goes straight to Miami. The divers who catch them are not paid enough to buy their own catch and barely even enough to buy other food to feed their families.'

Last year the divers in Bilwi, who have seen their rates of pay cut lower and lower, decided that they could no longer make a living from what they were being paid. 'The strike lasted fifteen days,' Hector sighs heavily. 'The Company held out, the divers had no choice so they had to go back to work and they were broken and hungry. The Company went ahead and reduced their rates further.'

Hector believes that only the big companies from Miami could force an increase in wages. 'This is something that they could do, yes, but you have to understand that in Nicaragua, everything happen "*baho de la mesa*" (under the table).'

Some idea of just how tough the daily grind is is brought home to me when I spend time on the *Promar*, a 100-foot junk, once white but now a grubby shade of diesel-exhaust grey. Sixty men are on board: 26 divers each paired with a dory man, along with six sailors, a cook and a captain. The captain is a stocky, heavy-moustached man from Honduras who welcomes me aboard with a rather formal and quite old-fashioned shake of the hand. After a quick inspection of my passport he tells me that he is happy to have me aboard and I'm welcome to catch a ride with him until he returns to shore back at Bilwi.

The boat is equipped for diving. There are two compressors either side of the deck which are capable of filling 150 tanks and secured next to a large pile of grubby fibreglass canoes near the rear of the boat. The boat will be at sea for ten days, with eight of those days spent diving. The first day will be spent getting out to the deep water where there's the best chance of finding lobster.

The *modus operandi* aboard the *Promar* is worse even than I'd seen on the Miskito Keys with Wally. A day at sea is divided into morning and afternoon sessions. In each session, the tanks are filled and the dory men ready the canoes. The lobster boat chugs steadily along while the captain uses a Global Positioning System to navigate along a channel 125 feet below. At regular intervals each canoe is lowered into the sea, and the dory man hops aboard and is handed down four tanks that he places on the floor of the dory. Once the dory is stable a diver jumps in and paddles over to it. Like Wally had done, the process of strapping on the rudimentary equipment and descending below the surface takes a matter of seconds.

As the divers have no depth gauges it's impossible to tell after their dives exactly how deep they have gone. Some US lobster companies concede that they can't always buy trap-caught lobster but insist that in such circumstances they only buy 'shallow-dive, hand-caught lobsters'. But it's clearly impossible to know what 'shallow-dive, hand-caught lobster' is. How can a company a thousand miles away know how deep these divers are going? The divers don't have gauges; they don't even know themselves.

In fact, every single diver can describe the floor of the channel to me, either being on it or near it, so I can see from the boat's GPS that they must have been diving in the range of 100 to 140 feet. In each session, a diver repeats that depth four or five times. Then, after a break for a lunch of fish and rice, they repeat the process in the afternoon. In total each diver will have completed up to ten sub-100-foot dives in a day. The youngest of the divers on board is just 15 years old.

The young men on board think they get a better deal than the divers on the Keys. The Company pays for all their food and their tanks. Eduardo, a 17-year-old boy from Esuera, tells me that this 'reduces the risks'. But what about the risk of one of them having a potentially fatal accident? 'We haven't had any accidents on this trip,' he tells me. 'But one of the older guys has got pains in his legs. See there? See him is limping.' I follow the line of his arm to the top deck where a young man is carrying his right leg, a clear sign that he is suffering from decompression sickness or 'the bends'. But despite his affliction, he has still dived every day of this trip.

Not all the boys on board are divers. Ernesto is one of the sailors who man the boat. 'All the young boys want to be divers around here. They say it easy money.' He exaggerates the 'easy' with a long Caribbean drawl. 'But sometime they come back dead or them bodies are all old from the pressure.' He demonstrates by contorting his wrists as though he has cramp. 'Better to be a sailor. Live longer.' He laughs a dark demonic laugh as he says this. He can't be much older than 20 but he has a darkness in his eyes that suggests that he's already seen real suffering.

Ernesto then hushes his voice as he continues. 'We come up from Bluefields, down the shore, this week. Captain take a call on the radio from another boat because them got a problem and so we stop the diving and we go. Boy from Bluefields, diver, come up from 150 feet all blood. Him all blood coming from out him nose and him ears. They pull him up on the dory and him chuckin' up blood too all in the dory. Not long. Not long 'cause him dead.' Ernesto shakes his head. 'Him boy from Bluefields, we all know him, him called Antonio, Antonio Willis.'

Just as life on the Keys is lived in fear of hurricanes, so too is life on the boat. With 26 divers under the water at any one time, a squall or storm blowing in can create chaos. Ernesto has seen this before. 'I seen plenty times when rain come and the dory man can't find the diver. They lost.' I'm astonished. Out here at sea, the idea of being stranded and unable to find the boat is terrifying. I've seen the movie *Open Water*. 'What happens when a diver is lost?' I ask. 'They sink to the bottom,' Ernesto says. His eyes widen again like saucers and he nods. 'I seen that plenty, plenty times.'

When the *Promar* has docked, the divers disembark and carry their bags towards the end of the pier where they are greeted by a mob of women. There is a perceptible buzz in the air as they chatter and gossip. At first I assume that, as this is a dock, the women might be prostitutes offering their services to the young men returning from a couple of lonely weeks at sea. But I am surprised to see that the money that is indeed changing hands is passing in the opposite direction to what I had assumed.

One of the women in the group is Albertina, around 40 and extremely striking. She is dressed in a grubby grey-brown A-line skirt and a faded pink vest, no jewellery, and wearing old flip-flops, her hair tied up in a neat ponytail.

Several of the ladies seem to be moving among the men and then returning to Albertina with information. With loud and clear instructions she begins pointing and passing money to them. Suddenly, she steps out of the crowd towards one of the divers and begins to berate him in quite aggressive tones. Try as he does to escape she will not let him pass until eventually she pushes him into a quiet corner adjacent to one of the wooden stalls where he passes her a bag. If I didn't know better, I'd swear I was watching a drug deal.

Albertina's husband was a diver before he died at sea nearly ten years previously. She was left to fend for herself and her three children. With no state social services to rely on she had to make a wage. Now she has carved out a niche for herself in the lobster market. She leads a sort of women's cooperative and has spotted an opportunity for making money.

By convention some lobster boat captains will allow their divers a modest personal allowance of lobster to take home at the end of a trip. It used to be that this lobster would be for the family pot as a celebratory 'Welcome home, Daddy' meal. But the price of lobster now makes this a luxury that most Nicaraguans cannot afford.

Fresh from 14 days at sea the men are desperate to hit the bars in town, but they have a problem: the captain doesn't pay them until he is paid by whichever company in town he sells the lobster to. This can take three or four days. If the divers were to sell their allowance to the company direct they might get paid a day earlier, but that doesn't help them buy beer now. Enter Albertina.

The women of Bilwi have worked out a way to exploit the divers' dilemma. The divers get paid around 70 cordobas (US$7) per pound on the boat by the captain, who in turn will get paid around 130 to 150 cordobas (US$13–15) by a processing company. The company doesn't care where the lobster comes from, so there's a clear gap for a middleman, or rather middlewoman, if she doesn't mind waiting a day or two for her return. Albertina and her team work the pier every time a boat comes in, picking up as much of the personal allowance of each individual diver as they can for

100 cordobas (US$10) per pound. When they're done they sell it to the Company for a juicy 30 to 50 per cent mark-up.

The divers are happy with the arrangement, sometimes even taking advance payments from Albertina or one of the other women before they leave. The man getting the earful just now was trying to renege on a prior arrangement until Albertina reminded him that not only had she already paid him but that she was a widow and he was stealing from her fatherless children – a reminder of how much the whole community has suffered.

Not everyone is having a tough time, though. At the end of the evening I spend with Wally and his family he announces that he is going to return to the shore to collect more provisions. Although he wants to remain longer on the Key, the Company boat that came from Bilwi yesterday with diesel for the compressor didn't bring enough rice or cigarettes. I jump at the chance to get a lift back to the mainland. Wally isn't going to Bilwi, but he'll happily drop me at Sandy Bay, further up the coast towards the border with Honduras, from where I should be able to hitch a lift home.

With the wind behind us, the sail back to the shore is considerably more comfortable than the journey out was. Wally rests serenely at the back of the boat, gently guiding the helm while scanning the waters for other boats. These waters are a motorway for cocaine traffickers from South America to the United States, and most of the cocaine that ends up in the US is shipped through here on speedboats, which the Miskitos call 'go-fast' boats, capable of carrying up to 2 tonnes of cocaine at a time.

It is estimated that several hundred go-fast boats pass from nearby Colombian territory through Nicaragua each year, at speeds of over 70 miles per hour. This is much faster than the top speeds of the patrol boats of Nicaragua's Atlantic Command, so the patrolling of these waters falls on the US Navy instead.

Many of the Miskitos see this war on drugs as an opportunity. Coastal communities benefit directly from providing support to the boats, either refuelling or providing refuge for the traffickers when the US patrol boats or helicopters spot them and give pursuit. Every Miskito has a story about someone they know finding a 'white lobster'. In the event that a go-fast boat can't avoid the patrols, the practice is to jettison the stash in 25-kilo waterproof parcels. With the cocaine sacks tossed overboard they simultaneously eliminate evidence and lighten the load so they can escape. Sea currents typically bring the discarded cocaine bales to the shore, and as often as twice a week one lucky Miskito fisherman or beachcomber wins the equivalent to the lottery. Each parcel is worth around $75,000 here, a huge sum of money to the Miskito people in the poorest region of the second-poorest country in the Western Hemisphere (after Haiti). Half of Nicaragua's 5.5 million people live on less than a dollar a day.

Rags-to-riches tales involving seaborne cocaine have become part of the local lore on the coast. Every Miskito I met had a story about a brother, an uncle or a cousin who had come into some money and sent for them to come and receive their share. But everyone speaks about one town, the islet called Sandy Bay. A Miskito-speaking community of a few hundred people, it has been transformed from wooden shacks and transistor radios to new solid brick houses complete with satellite dishes and widescreen TVs.

In Sandy Bay, cocaine money has been used to build new houses, schools and churches, in a project of self-directed development. It's just one of the many contradictions that the drug trade gives rise to. On the one hand, cocaine creates serious social problems; on the other hand, it brings riches. In the absence of other economic opportunities, is the cocaine trade a source of economic development?

Carlos Coffin, a preacher from Bilwi, works with the Miskito communities in Sandy Bay. I ask him whether he feels that cocaine has potentially done more in the local communities than the government. 'There is no question, my friend. None. Cocaine has definitely done more for these people than all the politicians in Managua. It is sad to say, but the drugs have made contributions. Look at the beautiful houses – they come from drugs. It is like a tax. The schools and churches are not built by the government. That money comes from the fishermen and their finds. Drug money has been used to build a school and replace the church roof. The pastors here get mad when they don't get their cut from the find. If a member of the congregation has found fifteen kilos, the church calculates fifteen times 3,500 dollars, that's 52,500 dollars, and at ten per cent they are saying: Where's God's 5,250 dollars?'

The Bilwi pier was built by one of the first US international corporations. United Fruit operated here back when Nicaragua was one of the original banana republics. The US fruit and timber company controlled the whole coast, filibustering and controlling governments, buying up huge tracts of land and planting bananas destined for the US market. They even built a railway line that ran all the way from the heart of the jungle to the end of the pier. Despite having ceased operations here many years ago, such was the connection between United Fruit and the Miskito region that the recent hurricane inspired United Fruit to donate $50,000 in aid to the Bilwi hospital.

In its pomp the pier ran a clear mile out to sea, but successive hurricanes, not least Hurricane Felix in 2007, have chipped away at it until today it is no more than a couple of hundred yards. Now its only tenants are the motley crew of old junks like the *Promar* and the occasional cargo ship.

One such ship is the *Captain D*, a converted 1942 US Navy coastguard boat that now runs frozen lobster tails and timber from Bilwi to the international port further along the coast at Rama. Its captain Norman Downs has agreed to give me a ride. Norman speaks good English, having been exiled to Florida after the war when the Sandinistas took over. He came back to Nicaragua in 1990 to reclaim various properties that the Sandinistas had commandeered illegally from him and resumed a life transporting cargo along the coast. He assures me his old boat is made of 'better steel still than any new boat'.

Norman is no stranger to the importance of lobster to these shores. It was he who first established the process of freezing fresh lobster tails for export from Bilwi back in the 1960s. Before that it all had to be shipped live to the United States via Panama. He ran a whole fleet out of Bilwi for years, making 'good money from it back in the days when it could still go for seventeen dollars per pound. Oh yes. Good money.' I put it to Norman that prices in US restaurants have gone up since those days but the price paid to the divers now is only a fraction of that. 'Well somebody getting rich then,' he replies with a ruefully raised eyebrow.

After his return, Arnoldo Alemán's new Liberal government approached Norman to invite him to become Minister of Fisheries. He jumped at the chance and came to the post with strong ideas. 'I said to them from the first day we got to do three things: first we got to stop the boats coming from Honduras into our waters and taking our lobster; second we got to stop altogether for three years to allow the stocks to build back up; and third we got to stop the crazy business of these boys diving for lobster and move to only using pots. Well, let me tell you, they did not like that in Managua one bit. I lasted three days before they bounced me back out.' The government was scared that these expensive policies might upset the US companies on whom they depend for business.

Norman's boat is now the largest boat that can still use the crumbling Bilwi pier. The government has decided that, rather than repair the pier, it would be better to build an international port at Rama down the coast, with Norman's *Captain D* acting as a shuttle between the two. We have to be in Rama by Wednesday with his consignment of lobster from the Carodi company in Bilwi in order to meet the big boat headed for Miami on Thursday morning. The Miami-bound boat acts as a collection point for lobster caught all along the shore from the Miskito Keys to Bilwi to Bluefields and the Corn Islands.

Norman's analysis and ideas are all sound. The systematic crippling of young Miskito men is, he believes, immoral. In an ideal world, there would be a wholesale move to trapping lobsters in pots – and possibly a moratorium on fishing to allow stocks to build up. In the real world it should at least be possible to make diving less dangerous. After all, divers around the world make multiple dives every day safely and with minimal injury by taking adequate precautions and employing safety techniques. These techniques could easily be taught to Miskito divers and enforced by boat captains. The problem is that money is needed for equipment and training. Who is going to pay for this?

Norman's view is that it is unrealistic to look to the Nicaraguan government to help here. The most powerful players in this supply chain are the US restaurants and seafood companies on whom the Nicaraguan suppliers depend. They are the companies who could most effectively bring about the necessary changes to the working conditions of the divers. After all, many of them openly espouse that new big business holy grail: corporate social responsibility. They do this partly because they are genuinely well intentioned, but inevitably they also do it for good business reasons. Putting it brutally, 'ethical' sells. The menus on the tables in Red Lobster Company, for example, proudly tell diners how the company has put millions into marine conservation so that the meal in front of them not only tastes good but also makes them feel good.

There's no mention of the Nicaraguan divers on the menus though. When questioned about this darker side of their supply chain, Bill Herzig, Darden's Senior Vice President of Purchasing and Supply Chain, said, 'Our product specifications make it clear we will not purchase dive-caught lobster. We only purchase trapped lobster that is harvested sustainably.'

Tragically, Miskito divers are caught in a world of double-think. 'We know deep-dive lobsters are wrong,' say the big companies, 'so we never knowingly buy them.' 'Since we never knowingly buy them,' the logic then seems to run, 'there can't be a problem to solve.'

It is, however, a hard claim to substantiate. One recent WWF audit puts the proportion of lobsters caught by divers taking life-threatening risks at great depths at more than 50 per cent. Statistically, it is inevitable that some will find their way on to the shelves or menus of an 'ethical' US company. There's simply no way to identify how a lobster was caught once it has been packed and shipped.

This is a classic example of the shortcomings of CSR. Some issues are certainly addressed, and companies gain competitive advantage from them. But many more go unnoticed or ignored. In the case of the Miskito divers, if the problem here was recognised, and if it was accepted that there are practical solutions close to hand, then much could be done with relatively little expense. On the other hand, there's always the drugs trade for divers to fall back on . . .

2

Keen to be green

UK: the ethical marketplace

'Well, we don't want to do dumb marketing'

Why exactly is the headquarters of McDonald's UK in East Finchley, a quiet suburb of north London? I put this question to Dean McKenna, head of McDonald's UK supply chain, as we sit down in his office. 'I think the guy who used to be in charge lived nearby,' he replies with an Antipodean drawl. 'Perhaps up in Hampstead.'

There's no doubt that having an office on your doorstep in London is very convenient. I also can't help thinking that being located in a rather anonymous-looking building well away from the centre of the capital is quite a good idea for a company that, let's face it, hasn't always enjoyed the best of reputations. There was a time when McDonald's wasn't exactly flavour of the month so far as the environmental movement was concerned, but standing in East Finchley's high street I find it hard to imagine hordes of demonstrators coming here to wave placards or stage a sit-in.

In 2005 the verdict on the final appeal against the ruling in the McDonald's versus Steel and Morris legal case was delivered. The case had lasted over 20 years. Steel and Morris were Greenpeace campaigners who had distributed leaflets alleging that McDonald's were engaged in activities that damaged the rainforest, were cruel to animals and exploited workers and children. The ensuing libel case and subsequent appeals amounted to the longest in British legal history. While McDonald's may eventually have won their case, it could fairly be described as a 'PR disaster'.

Clearly McDonald's has moved on a lot since then. Just as corporations like Starbucks and Nestlé have added ethically certified products to their portfolios in response to non-governmental organisation (NGO) campaigns against them, so McDonald's has been thinking the same way. A major rebranding exercise over the past four years has seen the company revolutionise the look of both its restaurants and its menu – cooler and greener, with salad.

McDonald's UK now source all of their beef from local British and Irish farmers, all their eggs are free range and the milk in their shakes is organic too. McDonald's has also changed its coffee-making so that it can serve the same kinds of lattes and cappuccinos as fashionable coffee shop chains such as Starbucks or Nero. 'We might be a bit slow getting into new things at McDonald's, but when we do, we tend to go 100 per cent all in,' says Dean. 'The old way was to serve only filter coffee, which was of variable quality, syrupy and bitter.' Dean smiles as he says this. Clearly, as someone who works here, he has first-hand experience.

However, a lot of work went into improving the quality of the coffee and at around the same time, in 2005, McDonald's also entered into an agreement with one of its sourcing companies, Kraft Foods, to buy all its coffee from more ethical sources. As of 2007, all the coffee sold in McDonald's restaurants has come from Rainforest Alliance-certified farms in South America. It's a major turnaround.

Rainforest Alliance, whose logo is a small green tree frog, is an NGO founded in the late 1980s. The company is based in New

York and works with farmers, large multinational corporations and small cooperative farms. As the name would suggest, it has a focus on sustainability of rainforests and environment. Most of the Rainforest Alliance's income comes from charitable donations; the Bill & Melinda Gates Foundation is listed as their top donor. They run several programmes aimed at sustainability in forestry, agriculture and tourism. One is a sustainable forestry division project called SmartWood, which encourages environmentally and socially responsible forestry. It has been praised in particular by Greenpeace for being the top scheme around: 'the only scheme truly developed in a balanced, multi-stakeholder manner and the only scheme to require "prior informed consent" of indigenous people in its standards.' (Greenpeace 2008)

What this means is that if you buy a coffee from McDonald's now, any and all of their coffee, all 1 million cups sold across Europe every day by them, comes from ethically certified sources. Next to the golden arches on the McDonald's styrofoam cup is the Rainforest Alliance logo. 'It used to be that walking down the street carrying a Starbucks cup said something about who you were,' says Dean. Now, it seems, the hope is that the same will be true of a McDonald's cup: it will say to everyone that you are an ethical coffee-drinker.

This is a smart move. When the Steel and Morris case hit McDonald's one of the main accusations levelled at them was that they were supporting irresponsible rainforest deforestation to produce cheap beef. What more convenient way to wipe it away than to place an ethical endorsement from the Rainforest Alliance on every coffee cup leaving every McDonald's restaurant in Europe? What better way to show everyone on the high street that McDonald's has put its past behind it and is now taking its corporate social responsibilities seriously? It's clever marketing. 'Well, we don't want to do dumb marketing,' smiles Dean.

Why the Rainforest Alliance? Why not, say, Fairtrade Foundation? Dean believes that the subtlety of the mechanical differences between Fairtrade Foundation and Rainforest Alliance are lost on most consumers and in fact McDonald's customers rely on and even trust McDonald's to 'do the groundwork' on their behalf, to suss out for them which is better. Actually Rainforest Alliance generates revenue in three main and almost equal ways: US government grants via USAID; certification fees and donations by private foundations; and corporate grants (such as that from Bill Gates). Yet Dean believes that Rainforest Alliance is a more market-driven system because it doesn't offer a fixed minimum price, making it a better alternative to Fairtrade Foundation. The strategy has certainly paid off. McDonald's has seen coffee sales rise 25 per cent since they made the switch.

There is an inevitable downside to this. McDonald's are certainly committed to paying a premium on top of the price of their coffee that can be used to fund socially responsible projects like, say, fixing some of the rainforests that they were accused of destroying. But because they are not guaranteeing a fixed minimum price, they will not suffer if the bottom suddenly drops out of the international coffee market. With the Rainforest Alliance model, if the price of coffee drops then so too does the price paid and there's no price floor to protect the producer.

There is something else nagging at the back of my mind as I talk to Dean. Ethical trade is clearly becoming big business: however sincere large corporations may be about why they are espousing these new ethical ideals, they clearly regard them as providing a useful competitive edge. The Red Lobster Company in the United States proudly boasts about its ethical credentials in every menu on every table in its restaurants, hoping to generate more customer loyalty; McDonald's signs up with the Rainforest Alliance and coffee sales jump by a quarter. Who could blame them? But I know from first-hand experience on the Miskito coast that the full picture is not always as rosy as it might seem at first. I can't help wondering whether all the encouraging things I am now being told necessarily stack up. And I can't help wondering whether anything gets lost when ethical trade becomes big business in itself.

My concern deepens when I visit the offices of a top London-based advertising agency involved in the ethical trade movement. Wieden+Kennedy occupy the kind of office I want to work in. At first I think I've walked into an amusement arcade, or perhaps a bicycle shop because there are at least 30 bikes in stands all around the edge of the reception area. At the other end of the room is a basketball ring and down the stairs there is a pinball machine and even a dartboard. I never worked in an office like this. Of course if I'd had an office like this then I would never actually have done any work, but then I never worked in advertising. Wieden+Kennedy has recently been employed by Fairtrade Foundation to coordinate their advertising strategy. Having a big agency on the books is evidence that Fairtrade Foundation is taking its branding very seriously.

Wieden+Kennedy is one of the most-awarded ad agencies in the world; it was *Adweek*'s 'Global Agency of the Year' in 2007 and has offices in New York as well as London, Tokyo and Shanghai. It is undoubtedly one of the world's coolest agencies, as the games arcade feel to the place testifies to. Just stop for a second to consider their name: it's 'Wieden+Kennedy', not 'Wieden and Kennedy'. Their literature proclaims that they create 'strong and provocative relationships between good companies and their consumers'. These 'good companies' include the *Guardian* newspaper and Save the Children, as well as Coca-Cola and Nike, for whom they coined the tagline 'Just Do It'.

They have heard I'm writing a book that touches on an area they have become particularly interested in – ethical consumerism – and so they've invited me to come to meet with them to hear my 'perspective'. I'm interested in hearing their perspective too, in particular how they plan to communicate the ethical consumer message to a wider audience. Many ethical brands have done very well over the past 20 years or so at attracting grass-roots campaigners, and their own research suggests that 75 per cent of consumers now recognise their logo. Recognition is one thing, but getting people actually to buy into it is another challenge altogether. Fairtrade Foundation in the UK, for example, is serious about expanding sales up to the point of having a 50 per cent market share in coffee, chocolate and tea by 2012, so there is a considerable amount of work to be done. In 2009 within the UK, proportionally by far the biggest fair-trade market in the world, the FAIRTRADE mark is still only on around 5 per cent of all coffee.

Four of the Wieden+Kennedy team have come to meet me and there is not a suit in sight. Sophie and Emma are responsible for managing the Fairtrade Foundation account. Sophie is a young woman, I would guess still in her 20s, and Emma is a little older, which is probably why I think maybe she's the boss, although I can't be sure. When your office has a Space Invaders machine in the corner, I'm not sure that the principle that used to apply in my office – oldest is in charge – necessarily holds true. The other two, Dan and Ray, are the 'creatives'. I'm pretty sure neither of them are in charge. It's their job to be creative, so I imagine being the boss would probably get in the way of that.

Up to now, Fairtrade Foundation has been extremely successful at increasing its awareness through grass-roots activities such as faith groups in schools, universities and even towns around the UK. Their members behave very much like campaigners, organising activities and events to expand the brand awareness. Fairtrade Foundation hasn't needed to advertise very much but, where it has, it has focused very heavily on one particular area, the 'Women's Press', i.e. magazines read by a key target group which Dan refers to as the 'Asda mums'. They are the key decision-makers in the household, the people who decide what does and does not find its way into the weekly shopping basket. Wieden+Kennedy's strategy relies on winning them over.

As we talk, it quickly becomes apparent that Dan has almost no understanding of the deeper issues at stake. Take, for example, a really basic economic principle like commodity prices: why do international coffee prices fluctuate? According to Dan, who is concerned about farmers in Third World countries receiving less for their produce than the cost of production, the reason for this lies to a large extent with the 'two for one' special promotions that supermarkets run. Dan assumes that to enable them to make special offers, distributors and wholesalers have to pass on the price squeezes to growers, which forces them to sell their produce for less than what is fair. In other words it is our demand as consumers for better deals at the supermarket that forces Third World farmers to sell their produce for less than the cost of producing it. Dan was a guest of the Fairtrade Foundation on a recent trip to the Windward Islands and this is what he says they explained to him.

It may sound persuasive, but it's also patently wrong. Prices for commodities such as coffee and sugar are set internationally. At the time of writing the sugar price in the world market is at a historic high of 23 cents per pound. This is not because individual agents are negotiating better deals for themselves, but rather because the Indian sugar harvest failed due to extreme weather conditions. India is such a big supplier globally that the result is a global shortage of sugar cane; when supply is low while demand remains high the market corrects by allowing the price to increase. If Asda in Basingstoke offers its customers two jars of NESCAFÉ for the price of one next week, it isn't going to affect the price of coffee any more than the price of eggs.

Obviously, for the 'Asda mums' who Dan is aiming to convince, these finer economic arguments are not important. Fairtrade Foundation is selling an ideal. It is selling guilt-free products that offer the kind of redemption equivalent to clearing up the mess the morning after a party. And, of course, in fairness to Dan, he is an advertising creative and not an economist. When he comes to create an ad for ethical coffee or bananas or sugar, he will focus on the positives: the smiling farmer, the new schools and wells built in the villages and the feel-good factor that comes with getting involved in ethical consumerism. Arguably, he doesn't need to understand the deeper issues.

Dan's perception is that consumers are lazy. They are already so attached to their favourite brands that they don't really want to give them up even if they do care. 'People just don't want to switch,' he tells me. 'They just think, "My tea is the best tea" or "My coffee is the best coffee", and because they already know these big companies like Cadbury or Nestlé, they don't want to have to feel as though they're making a compromise on quality.' The consumer, then, wants to feel more ethical, to show support for the poor farmer, but not if it means using an 'inferior' or lesser-known product. For big companies the answer is obvious: carry on producing what you produce, but if you can get a reassuring ethical logo on your product as well then you're ticking all the boxes.

The danger signs I picked up on at McDonald's are there again. On the one hand, we have consumers who want to do the right thing, but who don't have the time or inclination to find out what that right thing might be, and who assume that big business will take responsibility for that. On the other hand, we have companies knowing that ethical sells and queuing up to put the 'right' logo on their products. And we have the organisations behind these logos queuing up to build their 'brand', much as any ordinary company would do. But what happens if the slickly handled message doesn't quite stack up?

It takes a visit to the place where I grew up to confirm my suspicions. The number 11 bus that I took to school every day used to chug up the big hill in Bournville that runs past Cadbury's chocolate factory and stop briefly next to the pretty little cricket pitch outside the front. Twenty years later, I'm walking across that pitch on my way to the launch of the new Fairtrade-certified Cadbury Dairy Milk chocolate bar. In March 2009, Cadbury made the decision to change the way they source the ingredients for their best-selling flagship bar, the Dairy Milk. And that means that now any Dairy Milk bars in your lunchbox, corner shop or supermarket will have been made with ethically sourced cocoa and sugar.

This is a big deal for the British consumer because in the UK we collectively buy over 300 million Dairy Milk bars every year. It's hard to think of a shop in the land where you can't buy Dairy Milk and now the little green and blue FAIRTRADE logo will adorn the chocolates on the shelves of over 30,000 shops throughout the UK.

Cadbury currently sources all the cocoa for their Dairy Milk bar from Ghana. They switched production to Ghana 100 years ago as a protest against slavery. The Cadbury brothers who built the factory here in Bournville back in 1893 were instrumental in the fight against enforced human labour in the cocoa fields of Western Africa. When they could not obtain assurances from their suppliers in Côte d'Ivoire that their cocoa was being farmed without the use of slaves, they shifted production to neighbouring slavery-free Ghana and they've been there ever since. Today Cadbury are proud of this legacy – what could be considered one of the first acts of corporate social responsibility. And judging from the smiles on everyone's faces in the factory today, it would be fair to say they are just as proud of today's impending announcement.

Trevor Bond is Cadbury UK's managing director at this time. He is chairing today's meeting in the Cadbury boardroom in Bournville where a ragtag band of jobbing business journalists have assembled for a press conference. The group has been bolstered by a group of campaigners wearing black T-shirts emblazoned in large white capital letters spelling the word FAB. At first I pass this off as a Brummy fashion statement until it dawns on me that they are all from the Fairtrade Association of Birmingham (FAB) and they are positively beaming with pride in Trevor's direction as he delivers his well-rehearsed message. He's telling us all that today, in the midst of a recession, he has a 'good news' story for us. Today is a historic day; he is following in the ethical footsteps of the Cadbury brothers and he is sure that they would be proud of what he and the company are doing today.

Business journalists being what they are, the questions directed at Trevor are mostly focused on how the move to Fairtrade will affect costs and therefore profit margins. How will the shareholders react to the additional costs of Cadbury committing to

Fairtrade? Trevor reassures them in his most confident managing director's voice that the move won't have an impact on the company's profit margins because it's a long-term investment built into their business plan, just like TV advertising or marketing would be. He explains to us that the move into Fairtrade is an investment in Cadbury's future as a business.

Cadbury's concern is that the cocoa-growing industry in Ghana is in jeopardy because the next generation of Ghanaian children aren't following their parents into the business of cocoa farming. Instead they prefer to move to the city in search of more lucrative employment. Last year Cadbury commissioned its own research in Ghana. When 125 schoolchildren were asked whether they would go into farming, only three said they would. Alex Cole, Cadbury's former global corporate affairs director, explains to us that the rest actually laughed at the idea. So that is why, Alex says, Cadbury are taking these steps to invest in the future of Ghanaian farmers. There is a real fear that otherwise soon there will be no more Ghanaian cocoa farmers and – Alex pauses; it's clear she's been dying to deliver this line – 'without the beans there won't be the bars'.

A Dairy Milk bar is essentially made up of three ingredients: cocoa, sugar and milk. The deal that Cadbury has signed up to is to source the first two ingredients 'according to Fairtrade principles'. In the case of cocoa this means that they will honour the Fairtrade minimum price for cocoa of $1,600 per tonne, pay an additional 'Social Premium' of $150 per tonne on top of that and contribute to the costs in Ghana of farmers obtaining Fairtrade certification. Trevor's announcement is greeted with resounding enthusiasm by the assembled FAB members. Eyes are welling up; chests are filling with pride . . . 'Good on you!' one member cries out.

A member of FAB opens up to the group like a born-again Christian on a US television evangelism show about how she first saw the light of Fairtrade five years ago and how it has become her passion ever since. I suddenly have the strange sense of being at a cult meeting.

Alex Cole then tells the assembled crowd, 'This now means that Fairtrade will be on every shelf in every store and every person in Britain will become a Fairtrade consumer whether they believe in it or not.' Another FAB campaigner cries out his testimony: 'People never thought that they could change the world by sitting round drinking coffee and eating chocolate but apparently they can.' It's a big claim, and the cynic in me can't help thinking that changing the world may require a little more effort than eating even a few hundred million Fairtrade chocolate bars. Then Barbara Crowther, head of Policy and Communications for Fairtrade Foundation UK, floors me: 'This move can bring the joy back to cocoa farming.'

It sounds wonderful, if a little exaggerated, but let's look at the sums for a second. According to the International Cocoa Organization (ICCO), the daily price of cocoa on 20 July 2009 (the day that Cadbury launch their new scheme) is $2,939 per tonne. At the same time, the Fairtrade guaranteed price of cocoa is $1,600 per tonne, just over half the ICCO daily price. The price of cocoa would have to almost halve before the guarantee kicked in and the average Ghanaian cocoa farmer saw any benefit from the guarantee. Interestingly, Cadbury have offered no timescale to their commitment so only time will tell whether this situation will ever occur, or crucially whether they would stick by it if it does.

What about the costs of certification, which start at around $1,500 for a small cooperative? They are being borne by Cadbury.

So at least it's not costing the Ghanaian farmer any more to receive no more money; he'd probably feel less than joyous if it did. And so to the 'social premium'. The Fairtrade Foundation website states that the social premium is:

> Money paid on top of the Fairtrade minimum price that is invested in social, environmental and economic developmental projects, decided upon democratically by a committee of producers within the organisation or of workers on a plantation. (Fairtrade Foundation 2009)

The social premium is given to the farmers for 'collective investment'. It's up to them how they spend it. They could choose to build a water pump or a school or they could choose to improve their farms.

I like the sound of the social premium in the same way that I like the sound of Oxfam or Water Aid or any charity that takes donations to implement social improvements in developing countries. It's a form of aid and so, if used in the right way, it can make a massive difference to people's lives. The cynic might argue that this is aid, not ethical trading, but it's hard to argue with something that is making a direct positive contribution to people's lives.

Cadbury runs a charitable project called the Cadbury Cocoa Partnership. Over ten years, £45 million has been donated to cocoa-growing communities in Ghana, India and Indonesia in conjunction with the United Nations to invest in community projects like building schools. This would seem to be a clear altruistic act of corporate social responsibility, a genuinely sustainable initiative, and Cadbury continues to commit to it for the next ten years. So how does the move to Fairtrade compare?

As the market price of cocoa would have to drop by so much before the minimum Fairtrade price kicked in, it is unlikely that Cadbury will have to pay any more to the farmers in Ghana than they do already. What this move will cost them is the additional social premium of $150 per tonne on the 10,000 tonnes of Fairtrade cocoa for these new Dairy Milk bars. The thing is that the cost of cocoa doesn't really have much effect on the actual cost of the bar. An extra $150 on the tonne means 1.5 cents per 100 grams, which means that for a 49-gram Cadbury Dairy Milk bar, which is only 30 per cent cocoa, it's less than a quarter of one cent.

As I look around the room at the assembled journalists scribbling shorthand into their notepads, preparing to carry Trevor's 'good news' story to their editors for tomorrow's publication, I start to understand what he means about the move to Fairtrade being an investment just like marketing or advertising. Not many people have heard of the Cadbury Cocoa Partnership, which has cost them £4.5 million per year, but everyone is going to hear about their commitment to Fairtrade, and that is going to cost them considerably less.

I decide to go back to the beginning and arrange to visit one of the pioneers of the Fairtrade movement, and the father of ethical chocolate, Craig Sams, co-founder of Green & Black's (now owned by Cadbury, which is in turn owned by corporate food giant Kraft Foods). We meet up for tea in the garden of his Kent townhouse to discuss some of the background to decisions that Green & Black's took in their early years.

'When I started out in this business,' he reminisces, 'chocolate was still about getting laid – a mysterious man climbing through your bedroom window and all that crap.' It seems a long time since those Milk Tray ads but he remembers them well. In 1991 Craig founded Green & Black's, and three years later it became the very first brand to carry the FAIRTRADE logo in the United Kingdom.

Craig sips his tea and then continues in a languid Nebraskan drawl: 'Back then, we'd go to meet supermarket buyers and show them actual chocolate pods and they'd say "Wow".' His eyes widen as he remembers. 'They didn't even know that cocoa grew on trees in the shade of the rainforest. Certainly, nobody wanted to talk about the fact that there were a bunch of black people in raggedy clothes who were struggling to make enough to eat.' Of course that's all changed. Now the buyers travel and meet farmers all over the world. 'They know everything,' says Craig. 'And that's a huge injection of transparency – origin is hugely important in chocolate. People increasingly want to feel there is a link between the stuff they buy and something that they can identify with.'

Craig explains how Green & Black's became Fairtrade certified 'almost by default'. Because they were a small organic chocolate-making company, Green & Black's had been building relationships with small farmers in Togo and later Belize often on uncon-ventional terms. 'We had to convince these farmers in Belize to switch to organic and so we had to take them through the whole process. That meant we offered them rolling five-year contracts with guaranteed minimum prices as an enticement to ensure that they'd stick with it and we'd have organic cocoa next year. This happened to fall very neatly into the lap of Fairtrade Foundation. We weren't the reformed criminal that finds Jesus.'

In 1991 Fairtrade Foundation still hadn't found a product that they could certify in order to launch their own brand. 'They were close to signing a deal with Typhoo,' remembers Craig.

Unfortunately for them, the deal fell apart at the last minute. 'They were delighted to be able to turn to Green and Black's. Especially as we far exceeded the Fairtrade standards at the time. The only disappointment was that we were still only a piddly little chocolate company that most people hadn't heard of.'

Despite the small beginnings, this was the all-important start that Fairtrade needed. Craig too could see the benefits of the association with the Fairtrade campaigners. 'At the end of the day, we did it for marketing reasons and they had something real that they could go out and say to all their masses of supporters: "There is a Fairtrade product in the supermarkets – buy it!"' A rueful smile passes across Craig's face. 'The vicars got up in their pulpits and exhorted their congregations; at coffee mornings after church they were passing round bars of [Green & Black's] Maya Gold. We got a big boost from them and they got a big boost from us. Then we fell out.'

According to Craig, the end of the love affair came about for several reasons. 'They wanted too much for their administrative costs. They had crazy rules. They wanted two per cent then three per cent then four per cent. It's completely ass about face.' In fact the charges on wholesalers make up the lion's share of the income Fairtrade Foundation generates every year. The money paid by wholesalers to use the brand represents 90 per cent of Fairtrade Foundation UK's income stream, and around half of it is absorbed into the administrative costs of running and overseeing the certification process.

So does the other 50 per cent go to the farmers? No. The remainder goes into campaigning and promoting the Fairtrade brand. Fairtrade Foundation spends nearly half of all its income on promoting and advertising its own brand. And the figures suggest that it has been hugely successful in achieving its goals. Sales of

Fairtrade-labelled products in the UK reached almost £1 billion last year. Despite the recession, at a time when most retailers have been feeling the pinch, the past two years have seen Fairtrade-labelled sales continue to rise by over 20 per cent year on year.

Fairtrade Foundation UK makes no bones about its number one strategy being to increase its profile and its market share in the United Kingdom. 'We invest in community awareness,' explains Barbara Crowther from Fairtrade Foundation, 'to get people thinking about where products come from and how they can make a difference.' Fairtrade Foundation operates independently from FLO-CERT, the body that certifies and audits farms in the developing world. As far as Fairtrade Foundation UK is concerned, its job is to take money from UK businesses who carry its logo and then pump that money back into promoting the need for more UK businesses to carry its logo. The more businesses sign up, the more successful it is. So as well as attempting to draw new consumers to the Fairtrade label, the strategy has been to take the Fairtrade label to consumers by getting their favourite brands to sign up.

Craig says he wasn't happy with the Fairtrade approach. 'There was a point around 2000 when we would have taken the FAIRTRADE mark off the Maya Gold but you just can't take the mark off the pioneering product because it would have been impossible to put a spin on it that would have stood us in good stead. It would have been like the Pope renouncing Catholicism.' At the heart of his concern was a worry that as Fairtrade expanded its brand it would inevitably look beyond small cooperatives and certify more and more goods sourced from commercial plantations. 'All large-scale plantations are energy and carbon wasteful and inefficient in terms of productivity per hectare,' Craig says. 'A small farmer will generate twenty-seven times as much value out of a hectare as the largest industrial-scale ones, which can all be Fairtrade certified and can't be organic.'

Barbara Crowther accepts Craig's criticism, but points out that: 'Craig is prioritising the "organic" dimensions to ethical trade.' Fairtrade Foundation, she argues, are more interested in helping marginalised producers. She says that working with plantations was the only way to ensure Fairtrade's expansion: it enabled the Foundation to guarantee the kind of reliable, year-round volumes that the big retailers need. 'So, for example, with Sainsbury's,' she says, 'to get the kind of volumes we needed, we had to work with plantations. Smallholders alone wouldn't produce enough.' In other words, to pull the small farmers into the big supermarket deals, the plantations had to be brought in to bulk up the numbers. Barbara accepts that it is much harder to help the plantation workers: 'It's a very difficult situation to manage.'

Craig may not have been entirely happy with the Fairtrade approach, but, for their part, Fairtrade Foundation found that through Green & Black's they had finally established themselves. With Craig and co. signed up, Clipper Teas and Cafédirect quickly followed. Craig saw the inclusion of all these 'well-known' alternative trade organisations as completely necessary. 'If you don't get all the good guys to sign up, then people look at the FAIRTRADE mark on your packaging and think that you must be a bad guy who needs to be policed. Whereas Cafédirect are good guys who they can trust.' The strategy was clear – get all the good guys on board first and then you could more easily attract others later.

Barbara says that Fairtrade Foundation now have 4,000 Fairtrade-certified products on the UK shelves at any one time, and that they work with over 2,000 companies worldwide. Now most big brands on the high street have at least one of the products in their range ethically certified and labelled accordingly. Either there really are more 'good guys' out there these days, or the 'good guys' are just becoming harder to distinguish from the others.

That companies can make a powerful difference by actually doing the right thing rather than simply signing up to it is confirmed by a visit to David Keeper and Ian Meredith in their warehouse outside Gloucester, a visit that also confirms some of my misgivings about Fairtrade. When I arrive, Dave and Ian are happily engaged in a game of darts. 'We're in the middle of an important business meeting,' laughs Dave as I let myself in. Ethical Addictions is a UK company with the slogan, 'Not just doing things right, but doing the right thing!' Dave and Ian are the 'Chief Bean' and 'Head Bean' respectively.

'Our main customers are restaurants and coffee shops as well as a few hotels and farm shops,' explains Ian. The key to their business is that they can have direct contact with both their customers and their suppliers. Dave and Ian are middlemen trading not just in coffee, but also in information about who and where that coffee comes from, and how. Ethical Addictions has been running for only four years but already buys and sells over 20 different single-origin coffees from parts of Africa, Asia and Latin America. One of the coffees on their list is from a small village on the slopes of Mount Kilimanjaro called Orera.

'It's as good as anything coming out of Africa,' says Dave as he places a cup of Orera coffee down on the table in front of me as evidence. 'For us it's important to do the right thing – not just look like we're doing the right thing. We're not after a pat on the back and we don't want a sticker. We want to run a business and that means we have to make a profit. And so does the village. For the arrangement to be sustainable it has to be profitable right down the chain. That's the big sustainability picture, not the sticker.'

The Fairtrade minimum price for coffee in Tanzania is $2.81 per kilo. This is the price that a cooperative of coffee-growers registered with Fairtrade Foundation can charge if they sell the coffee with the Fairtrade sticker. But this is not the price that the farmers in Orera were receiving; they got less than half – only $1.38 per kilo, and in some of the other neighbouring villages less than $1. Ian found that much of the money going to the cooperative was getting swallowed up in administration costs, including wages paid to the headmen of the cooperative: 'For every 100 dollars that goes to the cooperative, as much as thirty or forty dollars can go to the elders.'

Ian and Dave decided to make a direct offer to the Orera villagers. Ian says he calculated that they could afford to pay US$4 per kilo (less 86 cents per kilo for milling to improve the quality) – still considerably more than the full Fairtrade price, and above market price at the time. But the villagers missed the point. 'They totally misunderstood,' laughs Ian. 'They thought we meant for a single bag, which they were still really happy about. We had to explain that we meant all the bags, not just one. Everything they had for four US dollars per kilo.' How did they react to that? 'They just all went quiet and sat there, staring at us in total silence. Stunned silence.'

Dave and Ian could have paid the lower price and made bumper profits but they didn't feel that fitted with their business model. The short-term profit-maximising approach would have been to screw the villagers and pocket the cash but Dave and Ian saw things differently. For them it was more important to encourage the village to become a long-term potential supplier of good coffee to fit their brand. If Dave and Ian are successful, there could be a lesson here for big business: only by taking the long view can you actually develop sustainable supplies.

Because Dave and Ian are buying coffee above the Fairtrade minimum price they could in theory put the FAIRTRADE logo on the packets of Orera coffee when they come to sell it. However, in order to do that, they would have to pay 2.4 per cent of the cost of the coffee to Fairtrade Foundation. 'What's the point of us paying them money?' asks Ian. 'None of that would go to the farmer.'

And here's the problem. Shopping for coffee in a supermarket, if I see the FAIRTRADE logo on one Tanzanian coffee bought from a Fairtrade-certified village and, next to it, Dave and Ian's Orera coffee with no ethical logo on it, if I didn't know better, I could easily believe that the Fairtrade coffee was the one that always offered farmers a better deal. In fact, the Orera experience shows that this is not always true. The primary cooperative, the Kilimanjaro Native Co-operative Union (KNCU), has large overheads. The actual amount going to the villagers is only half of what they found they could get by selling direct to Dave and Ian without any certification.

Of course, it just isn't feasible for ethical labelling organisations to individually certify every village. Working with cooperatives is the only practical way to operate such a system. But it's not ideal.

Dave says there's also a lot of misinformation out there about how the coffee business is run, which can affect consumers' decisions. Take, for instance, a statement on the Fairtrade Foundation website, which claims that:

The price of coffee has been struggling at an all-time low since 2000. It is way below the cost of producing the crop, leaving farmers throughout the world in crisis. (Fairtrade Foundation 2010)

International coffee prices as set by the New York market have actually been steadily rising since 2002 from $1.32 per kilo for the type of mild arabica beans grown in Tanzania to $3.38 per kilo by January 2010 when I was in Tanzania. At the time of writing, in January 2011, the price of mild arabica in New York has hit a whopping $5.73 per kilo. If there's anything 'historic' about international coffee prices then it is that they are at a historic high. The Fairtrade minimum is less than half of that, a mere $2.81 per kilo. With the exception of the three months during the global financial crisis in late 2008 following the collapse of Lehman Brothers, when all commodities took a brief dip, this minimum price hasn't been necessary for nearly five years.

When I drew this to their attention, Fairtrade Foundation accepted that, as coffee prices were indeed at a 13-year high, they would 'look into' updating their website accordingly. They said that the reference was to an old study from 2003/4. Out-of-date statistics aside, there is perhaps an important point to be made here. As with coffee, commodity prices for things like cocoa and sugar and tea are all at historic highs, and the minimum prices set by Fairtrade Foundation are all way below current market prices. This has been true for most of the past five years, which corresponds to exactly the same period of time in which the big corporates like Cadbury and Nestlé have signed up to the initiative. In other words, there's never been an easier time for big companies to sign up to Fairtrade, with actual prices being so much higher than the Fairtrade minimums. The consumer might think that companies are signing up to pay above market price. In fact – at current prices – they aren't.

There's another factor to be considered, too. Fairtrade Foundation does not require companies to formally agree that they will stick with the initiative. Any company can opt to drop the

FAIRTRADE logo without notice. Barbara Crowther says that neither Cadbury nor indeed any of the businesses currently carrying the FAIRTRADE logo on their products have signed contracts to tie them in long-term. 'We can't just say, "You must sign up for X number of years,"' she says. So for now, they can only try to 'stress the importance' of building long-term relationships. Trevor, for his part, says that Cadbury aren't only in it for the short term: 'You've got to believe that we're in this for the long haul.' Nevertheless the question that has to be asked is what will happen if and when things get tough, when commodity prices begin to fall again and the Fairtrade minimum price guarantees begin to kick in. At that point, carrying the ethical logo will start to cost a lot more and will begin to impact on profits and shareholders. I am not for a moment suggesting that a company like Cadbury would backtrack on their commitments, but there has to be a legitimate question as to what would happen in that scenario.

The idea of ethical certification came about in the coffee market when prices were low and organisations could make assurances about a few farmers and their livelihoods. But is it realistic for them to be able to make guarantees when they work with hundreds of major multinationals that make no such guarantees in return? And what's stopping these big companies from offering their own guarantees in the same way that, say, Dave and Ian do to their Ethical Addictions customers?

The impact that Fairtrade Foundation have had in stimulating the debate about whether business can play a greater role in development and sustainability is admirable and deserves credit. They have become the standard-bearer for the ethical movement and, as I saw in Birmingham, they have been influential in stimulating awareness of the issues at both grass-roots and boardroom levels. But somewhere in this, I can't help but feel that the existence of ethical labelling actually creates a disconnect between consumers and brands. Remember that Cadbury were running (and continue to run) a multimillion-pound sustainable initiative to help cooca farmers in Ghana, and did so long before their decision to sign up to Fairtrade. As a Cadbury customer, the year-on-year investment in the Cadbury Cocoa Partnership should be more important to me than logos and certifications from outside labelling organisations. Yet Cadbury must have decided that their message could be better represented to their customers by association with an outside ethical labelling organisation. And given the huge amount of positive PR that decision generated, you would have to conclude they were right. I can't help wishing, though, that Cadbury – excellent though their intentions are – were a little bit more like Dave and Ian.

So far I have focused on commodities such as coffee and chocolate, where there is now quite a venerable ethical history. But my findings in this area are not as reassuring as I had hoped, and they lead me to wonder about other types of trade and trades for which there is no ethical labelling. Much of the impetus for ethical business to date has been focused on such basic items as food and clothing, largely, I suspect, because these tend to come from what are very obviously the world's poorer nations (Africa, South America, parts of Asia and so on), where farmers and workers live on subsistence earnings and so desperately need some protection from the crueler aspects of international trade. But what about more sophisticated manufactured goods, which, after all, represent a far higher proportion of global business? Can we be confident when we buy a PC or an iPod or a new pair of running shoes that the brands we so quickly recognise are looking closely at how ethically their goods are being produced? I clearly need to look at this whole sector as well.

3

Bull in a china shop

China: the Pearl River Delta

'Designed in California, Assembled in China'

'Who knows the reason they jumped from those buildings? I wouldn't say that I am grateful to them, but we do get paid more money now.' Sitting on a concrete bollard just down the road from the factory where he works outside Shenzhen in southern China's manufacturing heartland, Zu drags slowly on a cigarette as he talks to me. His eyes rarely settle, flitting back and forth from me to the faces of the people filing past us. We have found a quiet place to talk, a little away from the roadside stalls offering cell phones and counterfeit branded T-shirts for sale. The street has turned into an impromptu market – the stallholders hoping to exploit the traffic of factory workers on the way back to their dormitories.

Zu has been working the daytime shift today, which means he started at 7 a.m. and finished at 5 p.m. Tomorrow he will start again at 7 a.m. That gives him 13 hours before he needs to clock in again. The quiet place where we sit is now beginning to feel uncomfortably crowded as more and more people file by. Zu suggests that we move somewhere else. 'Do you roller-skate?' he asks. 'I'm afraid not,' I tell him. He nods patiently. 'Well, we could go up to the square then. Lots of people hang out up there around this time.'

I stay close behind Zu so as not to lose him in the blur of the passing crowd. His gaze never rests, constantly surveying the faces passing the other way. Only once does he stop, to turn back towards a group of giggling girls who have briefly caught his eye. After 6 p.m. it begins to get dark. As we make our way further up the crowded street the lights on the stalls begin to flicker on and I'm reminded of being at a carnival or a music festival. Zu's hair is gelled up in the spiky style that is fashionable for teenage boys in China, and like all the other boys I can see he's still wearing the same jeans and white T-shirt that he wore to work. The girls are dressed identically except that their T-shirts are red. All carry the logo of the company that they work for – Foxconn.

In spring 2010 Foxconn made international news when, over the course of one month, 16 young men and women who worked at this factory jumped to their deaths. Some jumped straight from a factory window mid-shift, while others waited until they had returned to the dorm and jumped from their bedrooms. What strikes me immediately while standing outside this factory is the age of the workers – mostly in their late teens, around the age that Western kids are going to university or taking part-time jobs. I try to imagine the outcry if 16 teenagers working summer jobs at Walmart or Tesco jumped to their deaths in one month. Yet, despite being less familiar to Western consumers, Foxconn manufactures products for many brands just as well known on the high street: Apple, Nokia, Dell, HP, Sony, Microsoft and Nintendo, to name a few.

China now exports over $1 trillion of goods to the rest of the world annually. In just eight years, the size of US imports has more than tripled to $337 billion. That means that in 2008 China was producing over 16 per cent of all the goods passing through US customs (nearly 20 per cent if you exclude oil) – Walmart alone takes $18 billion of Chinese imports. The figures are similar for all the major industrialised nations of the world. The lion's share of this huge wave of products is made up of machinery, clothes and electronic goods made in Chinese factories by people like Zu. Yet most American or European or Australian or indeed Asian consumers have never heard of the companies making those goods because their names don't appear on the brands.

China has positioned itself as the assembly hub for global manufacturing. In 2008 over half of all Chinese exports were made from imported components. The *modus operandi* for most Western brands is to see that materials sourced in other parts of the developing world are shipped to China, where they can be processed, assembled, tested and packaged by Chinese workers.

The difficulty for the consumer wanting to judge the ethical credentials of their latest purchase is that the companies doing the producing are not the same as the companies doing the selling – just turn over your iPhone and look at the information on the back: 'Designed in California, Assembled in China'. The Apple logo makes clear whose brand you're buying, but no clue is given as to whose handiwork put it together. It's hard enough to trace the provenance of a coffee bean or a chocolate pod when it is sold directly by the farmer to you via one Western company. The ethical transparency of a phone is much more murky because its production is one extra step removed.

Foxconn generates more revenue per year than Apple, Dell or Microsoft. As well as producing several of the best-known brands of cell phones and laptops, it is the exclusive producer of Apple's newest must-have gizmo, the iPad. Its success is built on the company's ability to compete hard on price to win contracts. You need only look at Foxconn's profit margin – 4 per cent compared to Apple's 27 per cent – to understand that. The big bucks in the supply chain are still being made by the Western companies at the retail end.

So Foxconn's profits are created by increasing production volume – making only a few cents profit per unit doesn't look so good until you start producing millions and millions of units, then it starts to add up. Apple sold 60 million iPads in the first two months of sales in Europe and the United States. Retailers sold out of stock as customers queued for new deliveries. The pressure to make more units quickly became huge for Apple as well as Foxconn, and so the consequences of switching supplier simultaneously became unimaginable. With a contract such as iPad won, Foxconn have Apple locked in.

This is the shape of the twenty-first-century supply chain for manufactured goods. China has become the global factory because it can produce goods for a fraction of the cost of producing them at home. There's nothing new in the idea of outsourcing. Nearly every corner of the developing world that has cheap labour for sale has found Western customers happy to buy it up. But what is special about China is the scale of labour available and the quality and reliability of its labour force.

The processes behind making electronic gadgets such as the iPad require precise assembly and rigorous testing. There are several unique steps to be followed, which are not performed by machines but rather need to be done by human beings. The need to meet the demand for this kind of semi-skilled labour has prompted what has become the single largest human migration of all time. Within China over the past 30 years, four times as many people have upped sticks and relocated as during the whole of the nineteenth-century European migration to the USA. The vast majority of these new migrant workers are from the underdeveloped Chinese countryside. In China the phenomenon is known as *chuqu*, or 'going out', and refers to the young people who leave their villages looking for work in the factories of southern China. Today there are 130 million migrant workers in China. Foxconn alone has over 400,000 people working in their one factory at any one time. It's so large that it takes over half an hour to drive from one side of the factory grounds to the other.

Like nearly all of his 400,000 colleagues at Foxconn, Zu is a migrant worker. His story is a familiar one. He is the son of a farmer whose farm is in Henan, one of China's poorest provinces. After graduating from technical school at the age of 16 he realised that there was no work for him in the village, so he headed to Shenzhen and landed a job at Foxconn. Now he works on the assembly line, putting together laptops, iPads and iPhones.

As would any good Chinese son, Zu wires home a portion of his pay packet every month. The flows of money from migrant workers have been the main driver in the reduction of rural poverty in China. Tradition also sustains the system, as in China a young man cannot marry until his parents have built a house for him to live in with his new bride. Zu estimates that a wedding including dowry will cost his family 40,000 yuan (£4,000), and the same again for a house for him to live in. 'My family can never make that money from our farm,' he says with a shrug of the shoulders. So Zu and his three sisters have all 'gone out' to work in factories like this one, each sending money home every week until Zu can honour the family name and get hitched. 'I miss my home,' says Zu. 'Of course, I look forward to returning. But first I want to learn more things and experience something different.'

Zu's current job in the factory requires him to perform the same task around 10,000 times a day – equivalent to once every four seconds. Not surprisingly for a bright young man at the end of a shift like that, he seems a little on edge. He says he is becoming bothered by the repetitive nature of the work as well as the harsh conditions. 'We are forbidden to talk while we are working so it can be very lonely. Money is important but I would like to have a more interesting job. If you do well then you can progress. If I stay for two years then I could move to be supervisor of my station.'

After Zu's co-workers committed suicide, Foxconn raised the basic monthly salary from 900 yuan (£90) to 1,200 yuan (£120). If Zu works weekends (which he usually does), then he can earn 2,000 yuan (£200) in a month. Last year, when he was working on the iPad, he was earning £300 a month by doing 25 hours' overtime a week – the Chinese legal overtime limit is 36 hours a month but at Foxconn the overtime was compulsory. Not surprisingly, Zu says he was very tired during that time. Now he's more concerned that bigger changes are afoot. 'There is a rumour in the factory that Foxconn will move next year to Henan. If I want to carry on working for Foxconn then I will have to move too. I will be near to my home then but the wages in Henan will not be so high.'

Foxconn have indeed announced that a move to Henan is imminent. Before the suicides Foxconn had been flouting the legal minimum wage, which in Shenzhen is 1,100 yuan (£110) per month. The recent wage increase came after intense media scrutiny following the suicides. Companies like Apple and Dell were put under the microscope as their customers began to fear that they might somehow be indirectly responsible for what was going on in Foxconn. No doubt they in turn made Foxconn fully aware of that discomfort. Moving the factory out to Henan where the minimum wage is only 600 yuan (£60) has the additional advantage that Foxconn can continue its pledge to its customers that it will honour its minimum wage responsibilities and, at the same time, keep unit costs low by cutting the wage bill again potentially by as much as half. Apple have said that the move is 'enabling workers to be closer to their home provinces.'

For the big electronics companies using Foxconn, the wage rise was an important damage limitation exercise. The last thing major international companies like Apple and Sony want is to see their corporate image tarnished by association with a factory that had suicide issues.

Sony works hard in China to strengthen its reputation as a socially responsible business. After the Sichuan earthquake in 2008 it donated to the disaster relief fund, helping provide blackboards and desks to local schools destroyed by the quake. It has also been involved with a number of CSR 'initiatives' such as the Sony ExploraScience museum, which was built in Beijing. On its website, Sony describes the museum as 'an educative playground for both young children and adults'. The idea is to give young folk the opportunity to 'explore principles of science through practical experiment with the latest electronics'. Sony promises that 'many new gadgets are on hand for try outs'. I don't expect that Zu and his colleagues will be using up any of their rare days off to visit though. They've probably seen quite enough gadgets for one lifetime.

Asked about his company's reaction to the Foxconn suicides, Apple's Steve Jobs responded: 'Apple does one of the best jobs of any company in our industry, in fact in any industry, of understanding the working conditions in our supply chain.' He might be right, but if Apple is doing the best job of anyone, and yet still 16 teenagers on the assembly line take their own lives, what does that say about the rest?

Of course, you could argue that the responsibility for all this should fall at the door of the Chinese authorities. It's up to them, not foreign businesses, to regulate and put their house in order. A more pragmatic view might be that it's a shared responsibility. But while we argue about who is to blame, the problems inside the factory are only getting worse. A wage rise helps but is only temporary, and it merely papers over a major crack in China's economic development. Twenty years ago the migrants coming to look for work in the cities were illiterate farm workers, but China's ambitious policy of free, compulsory education in the countryside enforced over the past 20 years is beginning to change all that. What it means is that, while they are still flocking to the cities looking for work, China's rural poor are coming with an extra year or two of education, better qualifications and more ambition – ambition that cannot be matched by industries needing automatons to perform mindless repetitive tasks. It's not surprising that bright young people like Zu finally lose hope when a job means repeating the same task every four seconds, twelve hours a day, seven days a week, in total silence, for a return of a £50 wage packet.

NGOs are a little thin on the ground in China. One of the few to support stronger labour rights for migrant workers is headed by Mr Liu Kaiming, a former business journalist turned campaigner. He's a short thin man with short thinning hair and he explains in broken English why he took on such a difficult job: 'I was tired of seeing how migrant workers were being treated in their own country. We are supposed to respect the rights of the worker in China. That is what the country was built on, but now Chinese workers are second priority to the interests of big business.'

China's 130 million migrant workers are drawn from a total workforce of 737 million. Migrants compete mostly for manual jobs often without any written contract – simply a verbal promise of wages in return for work. One of Liu's daily challenges is aiding migrant workers who have fallen foul of one of the two-thirds of businesses whose owners offer no written contracts, even though the law requires them, and have rescinded on verbal agreements. Unfortunately the lack of contract makes it almost impossible for migrant workers to seek redress. His recent report collates data collected from over 800 factories and covers working pay and conditions for migrant workers. 'Many of them don't even pay overtime premiums. In fact,' he laughs ironically, 'many don't even pay the wages.' Chinese official estimates put outstanding back pay owed to migrants at over $12 billion.

Factory owners are under enormous pressure to keep costs down and at the same time raise ethical standards to appease their Western buyers. Liu has uncovered several instances of Chinese companies having one 'showcase' factory where conditions are excellent while running a number of 'shadow' factories where conditions don't reach basic standards and where illegal levels of overtime are routine. 'When the Western company comes to audit, the owner will show them the "showcase" factory to make them satisfied and then keep the other factory in the shadows where it cannot be seen. This is how they can keep the costs so low.'

In the West we might assume that China's central government would not stand for such behaviour, but the reality is that many labour laws passed by those at the top are never enforced. The reason, according to Liu, is that responsibility for enforcement falls to local officials and too often they are willing to turn a blind eye in return for a pay-off. 'Being a local government officer is seen by many young people as a way to get rich. Maybe even richer than a factory owner,' says Liu.

When it comes to the really big factories the problems become even more complex. Liu says that the bigger the factory the less the government looks into how it treats its workers. 'The problem is that companies like Foxconn are too important for the government to challenge them.' Last year Foxconn's electronics exports dwarfed all its rivals' and accounted for over 4 per cent of the total exports from China. That makes them China's number one exporter but they get such a large tax dispensation from the Chinese government that Foxconn aren't even in the top 100 corporate taxpayers in China and don't pay tax on imports at all. For their part, local governors are keen to encourage companies like Foxconn to open a factory in their district because the company creates so many jobs.

The global demand for Chinese-produced goods from companies like Foxconn continues to rise exponentially. Ironically what may help the worker is exactly what may hurt his bosses. China's one-child policy may be beginning to curtail the flow of young workers and soon even China's 1.3 billion population will no longer be able to meet the demand for cheap labour. 'We will soon have labour shortages in certain industries and then workers will have more power,' says Liu optimistically. Things are changing slowly for migrant workers but that's more down to simple economic forces of supply and demand than because anyone else is helping them.

In fact, several factors are working together. Labour shortages mean that workers can be choosier but, being better educated, the workforce is now looking not simply for money to send home but rather opportunities for self-improvement. As Zu and the other Foxconn workers I spoke to show, China's new generation of migrant workers want to earn while they learn. In the poorer districts of China the improvements made in education over the past 20 years are showing signs of dropping off as the number of school-leavers taking the *gaokao*, the national college entrance exam, has fallen by over half a million for the second year in a row. 'Children used to work hard to improve themselves because they thought it would help them to get a better job but now they realise that those jobs don't exist so they think getting a college education doesn't look like such a good investment any more. It all makes becoming a migrant worker seem more attractive.'

The fear for campaigners like Liu is where this shift will end. He has seen children as young as 13 'going out' to work in the cities, having given up completely on the idea of finishing school. The young rural poor in China are caught in an unenviable situation: they realise that continuing education will likely ultimately lead only to more frustration at the lack of opportunities in the future, while at the same time they can calculate that delaying starting work only delays the ultimate goal of earning enough money to afford a house back in the village near to their families. In rural China, education now has a negative utility value.

Liu sees a glimmer of hope for the migrants. First, this new generation of migrants are arriving in the cities better informed, having heard all the horror stories about unscrupulous bosses from older relatives who were migrant workers before them. And second, younger migrants are communicating with each other. 'The most important thing is the Internet,' says Liu. 'Slowly the migrant workers are finding ways to share information about what life is like inside the factories.' Although the Chinese government uses sophisticated firewalls to block social networking sites like Facebook and Twitter, more and more tech-savvy young Chinese are learning how to 'scale the wall'. It is the workers themselves who might ultimately bring about the transparency needed to create change.

Sitting in the student coffee shop at the University of Guangzhou, Mr Liang doesn't quite have the look of the average mature student. He wears an expensive polo shirt and a pair of designer jeans. He fidgets with the keys to his car, which, judging by the logo on the key ring, I guess is a BMW. Mr Liang is a mature student, however, but he is also a millionaire. When he left school 30 years ago he did so without a high-school diploma but still managed to go on to set up his own successful business empire in China's manufacturing heartland. His company produces aluminium windows, doors and shelving for factories and warehouses.

Mr Liang's factory is fairly typical of the sort found in the cities of southern China. He employs around 500 people, mostly migrants. His success is built on his ability to produce aluminium products for a fraction of the cost that his US competitors charge. This is thanks in part to the lower rents but mainly the low cost of migrants.

Mr Liang has been finding good labour hard to come by of late, and that is beginning to have an impact on his business. 'My migrant workers want to do more and more overtime. We have to tell them we can't afford it sometimes. But it is more expensive to find and train a new worker so we must find a balance.' Another part of that balance is the conditions that the workers enjoy in the factory as well as the dormitories and canteen provided by Mr Liang.

China is unique in respect of the extent of the connection between worker and employer. Chinese companies have a unique responsibility for their workers because, with most workers being migrants from other parts of the country, the company is responsible not just for the conditions on the shop floor but also the living conditions when the working day is done. Migrant workers need to be fed and sheltered. For many migrants that means the factory provides a framework for their whole lives. In the worst-case scenario a migrant worker might have to suffer poor working conditions during the day and put up with bad food and a lumpy bed afterwards. For this reason, Chinese companies must take their social responsibilities very seriously.

'Most workers' eyes are sharp,' says Mr Liang. He feels that if a migrant thinks they can find better digs down the road then they will move. 'We want to pay more attention to facilities, but it's about talent not just facilities.' However, when Mr Liang says 'talent' he doesn't mean his ordinary workers. Last year he invested some large sums of money to attract two university professors from the design and engineering departments to work with him. He believes their reputations will help to enhance his own brand. He doesn't believe his customers care so much about his other workers.

'There are no secrets in the industry,' he goes on. 'We know what the facilities are like in our competitors' factories, and so do the workers.' This could at first glance be interpreted as a good thing, as workers can exercise a choice. Unfortunately, in reality it merely provides an incentive for factories to keep things as they are until there is a need to improve. If one factory were to put in a new canteen then the other factories would have to follow suit, but until that happens they can all carry on as normal with their old canteens. Mr Liang is doing just that – improvements are planned, but until they are required they won't be implemented. Better to spend the money attracting professors.

His association with the university prompted Mr Liang to follow a programme of his own self-development. He has enrolled in courses to learn English and ancient Chinese philosophy. 'I realised that if I do a little work on myself then my business will grow even more. I'm reaching my inner world. What did the generation before me leave for themselves after they'd worked so hard?' He would not see investing in such courses for his migrant workers to reach their own 'inner world' as a similarly shrewd investment. 'How could I be sure that they would not just leave to work somewhere else?' he asks.

I leave Mr Liang and dash across town to meet an even more successful product of China's economic miracle. It's 10 p.m. and Mr Yu Pengnian is at his office in the centre of downtown Guangzhou, negotiating hard over the final details of a real estate contract. Mr Yu drives a hard bargain; the three people on the other side of his large desk are half his age but, judging from the expressions on their faces, they are having a difficult time. As a man who has made it on to the Chinese Rich List every year since its inception, he takes no prisoners when it comes to business. And at 83 years of age, he's seen it all before. When the deal is done, at nearly 11 p.m., he looks pleased. After he has meticulously stamped every page of the contract with his seal – nobody is going to pull a fast one on Mr Yu – the business is over for the day and he has time to talk.

This is the first time I have met someone with his own skyscraper. We are sitting in Mr Yu's office on the 58th floor, high above the bustling streets of Guangzhou's shopping district. The walls of Mr Yu's office are covered in framed photographs of him shaking hands with various senior Chinese politicians. Outside, the sky has a red glow from the Cartier and Porsche advertising billboards below, but there is nothing so modern about Mr Yu, who wears the traditional Chinese suit of the kind often worn by Chairman Mao. What sets him apart from the great dictator is the distinctive shock of jet-black hair backcombed into a quiff that would give Elvis Presley a run for his money.

During a period of exile from mainland China, which lasted over 30 years, Mr Yu made his first fortune from property deals in Hong Kong. 'If it wasn't for Den Xao and the "opening up" then I couldn't come back to the mainland,' he says as he flicks through a photographic biography of his life. He finds the page he's looking for and turns the book around to show me a picture taken 30 years previously. The picture shows a younger Mr Yu standing in front of a row of ambulances. His first act on his return from Hong Kong was to donate a whole fleet of emergency vehicles to the hospital in his hometown. The book is full of similar photos.

Mr Yu has a refreshing candour about how his acts of philanthropy have helped him to win favour with government officials, which in turn has helped him to make more money. 'Business is a circle. When I give money to a good cause in an undeveloped area then it comes back to me as goodwill from the local government. That might then help me to push through a real estate deal in that area. It's hard to say whether the company's motivations are to enhance reputation or to do good.' Mr Yu shrugs as if to say that he doesn't really care.

But Mr Yu wouldn't countenance giving money directly to government to allocate to those areas most in need. He doesn't trust government in China enough. 'I like to give money directly to the poor,' he explains. 'That way I know how the money is being spent.' There is much scepticism in China that money donated via the government doesn't reach the intended cause. Examples of this can be found in recent allegations filed by NGOs working in China alleging that Sichuan earthquake relief funds were seized and misappropriated by corrupt officials. Mr Yu looks at me earnestly and puts his hand flat across his chest. 'The money I've earned, I earned from the people and so I want to give back.' He nods to ensure I follow and then breaks into a chuckle for a moment before he adds, 'Of course, I have to make the money before I can give it away.'

The explosion of capitalism since the 'opening up' policy of Deng Xao saw a similar explosion in overnight millionaires: China had over 477,000 US dollar millionaires at the end of 2009, up 31 per cent from the previous year and trailing only the United States, Japan and Germany. But compared to philanthropy displayed in the West, Chinese millionaires' donations are still relatively small. Mr Yu aside, China's super-rich increasingly prefer to keep it for themselves. In 2009, a government-sponsored philanthropy league table listed 121 Chinese philanthropists. Their combined donation came to $277 million, less than half of what American financier Stanley Druckenmiller and his wife gave away in the same year in the United States.

Mr Yu doesn't believe that many of the next crop of successful Chinese businessmen share his vision either. 'My experience is a little different because my company has no board of directors – so what my company does is up to me.' China is developing into a broader capitalist economy where the big companies do have boards of directors and institutional shareholders. 'The next generation are totally different,' says Mr Yu. 'If there are many stakeholders then there are disputes. And the young generation are not so responsible so they focus only on making money and not on doing good.' He nods his head at me with a sad resigned look, as if this is something that he has clearly thought about before.

If Mr Yu is to be believed then Zu and the other migrant workers have few friends to turn to in the business community in China. Whatever goodwill existed in the older generation of businessmen is dying off; what little remains is still manifested by way of individuals making private donations rather than any true form of sustainable corporate social responsibility. And that isn't a concept that Chinese-owned businesses are in a hurry to embrace.

Perhaps this reflects the nub of the problem with working conditions in China. Despite the Communist tag, China is a culture of fierce individualism. There are few places on earth that could claim to be less Communist in this regard. Add to that a government that increasingly acts to favour the interest of business owners over workers and you have a recipe for a dysfunctional society with little or no social responsibility. How can the migrants turn to the government for support when it is so easy for corrupt bosses to get the government off their backs by writing a cheque for whatever pet project of whichever influential politician they are trying to influence? How can the workers hope that the kinds of initiatives needed are going to come from their government when they can be paid off by the other side?

This is frustrating, as China is a country where things tend to get done once the government really wants them done. Maybe what they are waiting for is sufficient pressure to force them to respond.

During 2010 there has been a massive rise in the number of industrial disputes in China. Much of the media attention focused on foreign companies like Foxconn and Honda, but there were an estimated 100,000 demonstrations nationwide in 12 months. So far there has been no big crackdown on worker activism but neither has any clear labour activist leader yet emerged. There is little history of trade unionism in China and until now workers have remained largely ignorant of their rights and entitlements, but demonstrations suggest that things are changing and it should be a cause of concern for the Chinese government.

As Mr Liang says, workers' eyes are sharp, and the more awareness they gain of their audience in the West the more likely they will be to begin to find the courage to challenge their bosses.

If their resentment is ever collectivised into an effective social movement in the same way as in Poland during Soviet times, for example, then things may begin to really hot up. They say in China that every government minister knows one word of Polish: '*Solidarnosc*'.

I am beginning to wonder whether anyone in China other than the last remaining Chinese philanthropist will actually engage with the human misery being caused by the country's rapid economic expansion, when I finally manage to pin down Bill Valentino. I have been trying to do just that for the whole time I've been in China because his name has been mentioned several times during my visit. But it's only towards the end of my stay that I finally manage to get to talk to him in his kitchen at home in Beijing. What's remarkable about this is that I'm in Shanghai. It's a sign of the times and the way business is being done in China today that we're talking face to face over Skype at nearly midnight. I'm beginning to realise that, like nearly everyone else I've met in China, Bill is a busy man.

The news today has been filled with stories from the BP oil disaster and we are discussing the perception in China of the likely effect on their reputation. 'All the Chinese people I work with were saying, "But they're such a good company and they do some much good for the environment . . ."' It's true that BP do tremendous work in the environment, but of course even the mighty can fall and their great reputation didn't stop BP making a really costly error. Bill agrees: 'Any company at the highest pinnacle of corporate social responsibility can fall very quickly to the lowest point if they don't see it as a strategic part of doing business.'

Bill is a North American who has been working with several

foreign-owned businesses within China to find ways to improve their CSR programmes while simultaneously creating value. He is currently employed by German chemical and pharmaceutical giant Bayer. He says there's no point in even talking about trying to encourage businesses in China to change their behaviour unless they can be convinced first to create value, in particular economic value.

He talks enthusiastically about where he's coming from: 'You have to be talking about how change is going to build a better brand or reputation or attract better employees, or it's going to mitigate risk in your supply chain. Because true CSR needs to be measured over the long term. If you're looking for short-term results then it's probably just PR.' For Bill, donating blackboards doesn't count; the crucial issue in China is all about creating stability.

'Here CSR is focused on environment, but also on poverty reduction, health and education – what we call "capacity building of civil society".' Bill thinks that all this feeds neatly into a very Chinese cultural need for stability in all things that goes back to the ideas of Confucius. 'They call it harmony or balance.' He believes that this need for balance is being felt in China now more than ever after the phenomenal economic growth of the past 30 years, 'because what went with that growth was phenomenal neglect of environment and social development'. In other words, China's yin and yang are out of kilter.

Since 2007 all Chinese state-owned enterprises have been given strict rules for CSR. The problem is that they have no idea how to implement it. Bill believes there is a very unique Western mindset that sees a problem and then thinks creatively about how to solve it. 'The problem in China is that they are incredibly practical. They are instinctively left-brained. Look at the upper echelons of the

Chinese Communist government and it's made up of over ninety per cent engineers and military. But to come up with creative solutions to problems, you need to use the right brain which is where design and empathy and storytelling and having fun in what you do come in.'

Bill is keen to show me examples of how he has helped Bayer to make money and simultaneously create social value in China. His thought process is definitely right-brained: 'Many people think that enlightened self-interest is a bad thing and that it means you're only thinking of yourself, but if you're doing something that is creating environmental or social value then you have the right to say, "I have the right to make profits and to create wealth for my stockholders."' This is not a view that is particularly at odds with what Mr Yu has been doing for the past 20 years. But Bill wants to take it further, and that means getting away from the idea that corporate social responsibility is just another form of PR. Most companies are still more interested in getting a short-term boost to their reputation rather than creating long-term value from CSR. They just can't shake that idea when actually they need to think more strategically.

In 2002 Bill proposed to Bayer that they roll out a programme of micro-financing, giving loans to farmers in some of the same poor rural areas of China that the workers I'd met at Foxconn hail from. Initially he met with some resistance from his employers. 'They were saying, "What the hell are you proposing? We're not a bank, we're a chemical company."' Bill smiles broadly, as if he's remembering their faces. He obviously enjoyed the challenge, probably because he was thinking strategically. 'One of our biggest stakeholders in China is the agriculture sector. But the poor farmers in western China can't afford to buy our products.' Bill identified that there might be a huge potential market for Bayer products such as fertilisers and pesticides but that the farmers at the bottom of the pyramid were still existing on subsistence farming with no funds even to consider buying these kinds of products. No one knew how big the potential was here, but Bill's argument was that by getting involved in the community it would allow Bayer an opportunity to learn more about the market.

'Now we are able to ask the farmers in the communities what they want. We're not just coming in and building them a school or a church or giving the local chief a couple of Mercedes. We are responding to the community's need to improve their livelihoods. And then while you're giving farmers loans you can also teach them how to use pesticides safely and efficiently. Of course, then the Ministry of Agriculture get involved because they like what we're doing.' And that's the all-important piece in Bill's enlightened self-interest strategy, because the Chinese government are also one of Bayer's most important stakeholders as they are required to license all of Bayer's new products in China.

Bill is quick to point out that he never sees it as business's responsibility to eliminate poverty but he sees that they can have a role in building models that lead the way. By showing how things can be done through their core business and by providing the initial investment they are able to encourage government and NGOs to become involved where they might not have thought to previously.

'So we start with an experiment like micro-financing and with the idea of creating agricultural livelihoods and then we connect to healthcare and everything that surrounds poverty like education and the environment and then we see if can we scale this to a whole district.' At this Bill holds up his hands and admits that the district Bayer chose – Chongqing – was very strategically selected. Being one of China's poorest districts and having recently suffered an epidemic of organised crime it had become a thorn in the side of the Chinese government. At the time, one of China's rising political stars and potentially a future leader – Bo Xilai – had been sent down there to sort out the mess. Bayer could recognise that Mr Bo was a good man to get in with.

To convince his bosses at Bayer, Bill was careful not to talk about any strategy to alleviate poverty, preferring to focus on the upside of the scheme of making important political connections and creating new markets. 'They don't want to hear about alleviating poverty. Better to talk about the economics and making money first so that they see the self-interest. Then with your last breath you can talk about creating social value.'

Bill sees many companies trying to put themselves forward as what he describes as 'the demigods of CSR', but he doesn't see any evidence of it. 'Maybe Timberland or Patagonia,' he offers as examples of companies doing incredible things, 'but for most companies it's an evolution. And it's settled in a department where some people are trying to do something good but most people in the company couldn't care less.' He sees that as the biggest challenge for companies operating in markets like China – how to encourage the dialogue within companies so that the need to make money can be reconciled with the need to create social value. 'The question is, how can you plan that? Where do you as a company find your intersect with society?'

There don't seem to be many mindsets of that kind in evidence in China. The lateral thinking of the kind Bill has, and which is so needed to find that intersect, has not been developed here, so it relies on Westerners to lead the way. Bill is hopeful and excited: 'The Chinese realise that they can't survive on the mindset they have. But they are concentrating on how to be more creative and more resourceful because they have the greatest problems in this country. Here you have the biggest problems and they need to be solved quickly. It's a great place to be trying out new ideas.'

At whose door does this leave the responsibility for change? A government reluctant to upset business leaders is more inclined to leave business to legislate itself. If Mr Yu is to be believed, the will to make the necessary changes is unlikely to come from within China. And according to Bill, even if the will was there, the ability may take some time to develop. So, for now, the best hope is that Western companies outsourcing to Chinese companies will push the social agenda. That means thinking creatively about how to ensure that conditions improve. As things stand, many talk the talk, but the evidence that they are actively working to change things is thin on the ground. Sixteen suicides are testament to that.

4

Rubber-stamped

Laos: Luang Namtha province

'They gave each of the villagers 800 American dollars and told them to get out of here'

Place your bets! The croupier pings the bell to bring to an end the flurry of banknotes and betting chips hurriedly being flung on to the baccarat table. She reaches over to the large stacked deck of cards, discards the top one and then lays another two on the table. The first she places carefully in front of a Chinese dragon symbol and the second next to the Chinese symbol for a tiger. The game is simple – to bet on which card will be higher. 'The Chinese like to keep their betting games simple,' explains Robert, a former Russian weightlifter, who is fluent in Chinese (and, fortunately for me, English) and employed by the casino as a translator. 'And they also like to work together. Look how everyone is gathered around this one table when there are plenty of empty tables in the room.'

It seems that the Chinese gamblers around the table also like to back a winner. One man in particular is betting big. He has 10,000 yuan (around £1,000) placed strategically on the dragon square. He's betting that in the next round the dragon card will be higher than the tiger, and every other punter around the table has followed his lead. The croupier slides what looks like a fish-slice under the dragon card and pushes it face down towards the man; as the star of the show he gets to reveal the result. In front of him, at the end of the table, Chinese banknotes and casino chips are piled up on the dragon square while the tiger square at the other end remains empty. The croupier goes first and overturns the tiger card – nine of clubs. All attention turns back to the man at the end of the table.

The man places his right hand flat on top of the dragon card and then with his left hand he slowly begins to peel back the edge, millimetre by millimetre – in a Western casino this would be totally unacceptable as the card will be marked permanently, but here it seems to be part of the drama. Eventually a sliver of black is visible in the corner – enough for everyone to recognise that it's a face card. Triumphantly he turns it all the way over and slams it down on the felt with a flourish, much to the joy and amusement of the onlookers. He has won and so they have too. While the croupier counts out the winnings, the crowd are already watching to see where their hero will place his next bet.

This casino is one of several in the town of Boten, attached to a luxury hotel where guests are greeted at the check-in desk with a deferential '*Ni hao*' – 'Hello' in formal Mandarin Chinese. What is remarkable is that this hotel and this casino are not in China. Boten is actually in neighbouring Laos. Gambling is illegal in China but not here. Investment has flooded into the town to build casinos and luxury hotels for Chinese punters. Investors in Boten are banking on it becoming the next Maccau. In anticipation of its success, the whole town and its surroundings have been leased from the Lao government for 30 years, with an option for another 30. And it's not the only land that's been leased out by the Lao government: in the area surrounding Boten, thousands of acres of forest have been sold off for agricultural development.

Despite being firmly within the borders of Laos, there is nothing remotely Lao about Boten. The town's road signs are all in Chinese, staff in the hotels speak only Mandarin and the town's main strip is a line of Chinese food stalls selling dumplings and fried duck. 'This used to be just a crappy Lao village,' says Robert. 'They gave each of the villagers around 800 American dollars and told them to get out of here. Since then it's basically a Chinese town.'

And to run a Chinese town, Boten has imported a Chinese workforce. In Robert's casino, fewer than 20 per cent of the staff are Lao and those that are can take only the most menial of jobs, as cleaners and porters. The public face on show is 100 per cent Chinese, which is never more in evidence than at 5 p.m., as the sun begins to set and a particular group of Chinese migrant workers comes on shift. The road opposite the hotel slowly fills with young Chinese girls. By 5.30 there are 70 or more girls, mostly in their teens, strutting up and down the hotel driveway pushing business cards into the hands of much older Chinese men. Each card bears the same phone number on the front and a unique identifying two-digit number on the back. If a girl takes your fancy then you have only to call and quote the number on the back of the card and she will be delivered to your door like an X-rated Chinese take-away. The hotel doesn't object and girls are free to come and go through the night – deliveries for the lucky punters with winnings to blow as well as for the unlucky ones whose chips are down but not quite out.

I have crossed the border into Laos from southern China. My time in China has opened my eyes to the significance its industries now have for the rest of the world. And I suspect that, just as this economic leap forward has not been entirely beneficial for the Chinese themselves, it may also not be unbridled good news for the countries who feed China's factories with the raw materials they so desperately need.

*

'Lao people like Chinese people. They bring good business, cheap motorbikes. Lao people like this.' This seems slightly at odds with my taxi driver Ken's previous tirade about all the motorbikes that pack out Vientienne's rush hour. For most of the 16 kilometres out of the city, through the suburbs and further towards the city's new stadium, we are flanked by a squadron of Chinese-manufactured mopeds and scooters.

As the traffic begins to thin out, we reach the national stadium – four colossal buildings stand proudly before us. As well as the running track there's a football stadium, a swimming centre and a gymnasium that gleams in the low evening sunlight. The complex looks so imposing that Ken is a little unsure whether we are even permitted to enter, but after some reassurances from me he agrees to drive through the gate and into the deserted car park. We pull up next to the main stand where a 20-foot-high golden torch stands proudly, distinguished and extinguished. There is no one here.

Ken follows me up the steps and through the open gateway to the stand. It's a little like going to the cup final at Wembley, give or take 80,000 people. We are totally alone and have the run of the place; only a low barrier stands between me and the running track where Suryo Agung Wibowo of Indonesia won the ASEAN Games 100-metre final in December 2009. I am all set to do a lap (just for fun) when I hear voices behind me.

Mani Sung and her three sisters have walked from their nearby village to the stadium to collect the vegetable pak bong, which grows wild in between the deserted parking bays. 'During the games, there were many many people here,' says Mani, 'but now, there's no one. Only sometimes when some companies hire the pitch for a corporate game. No one ever comes to watch.'

I wonder if she might have chosen to spend the money on

something else, a school or a hospital perhaps. 'I don't know about that,' she ponders, 'but I would at least have had a plan. People should come here every week to watch sports. Then we could all make some money.'

The stadium was a 'gift' from the Chinese government – a development project designed to raise the profile of Laos in the region. This is a common Chinese development strategy. Similar projects include cricket stadiums built in the Caribbean and football pitches in Latin America. Here in Laos, China is working hard to show that their investment is easy to rely on. The leaders of the two countries met over 20 times last year. As well as signing contracts to build large stadiums, the meetings address how Chinese companies can secure exploration rights to Lao land for hydropower, mining and rubber.

Built on the banks of the Tha river, Luang Namtha has a decidedly more Lao feel about it, albeit that it has become a stopover for Western tourists either making the overland journey to China or using the town as a base for treks to visit the ethnic tribes living in its surrounding countryside.

The Luang Namtha district has an estimated 18 different ethnic communities. Several eco-tourism agencies have sprung up in the town, having spotted an opportunity to sell 'hill tribe treks' to socially inquisitive backpackers interested in observing the unique tribes in situ. The agencies are flourishing since the government made it illegal for tourists to visit independently; the reason given was that the government wanted to protect the tribes by ensuring that tourists did not inadvertently perform social faux pas that might offend the tribespeople.

What the tourist guidebooks don't draw their readers' attention to are the low-rise office blocks dotted around the town, which belong to Chinese rubber companies. Over the border, in southern China, Yunnan province is the centre of the world's rubber processing industry. Last year Yunnan factories processed over 2 million tonnes of rubber latex for the production of everything from Bridgestone car tyres to Nike trainers. Demand is growing so rapidly that the Chinese government estimates that it will double processed rubber output before 2020 to over 4 million tonnes. The problem is that there is no room left in Yunnan to grow more raw rubber and so Chinese companies are beginning to look elsewhere.

The companies have identified Laos as a potential supplier of the shortfall. In particular, they have targeted the northern provinces, such as Luang Namtha, which geographically speaking most closely resemble Yunnan. Ruifeng Rubber, Yunnan Rubber and Sino-Lao Rubber are just three Chinese companies with a very visible presence in town. The boss of Ruifeng has arrived in town this morning. His brand new Toyota Hilux parked outside his house sticks out a mile in a town where most people can only afford a motorbike. A group of Chinese men sit on his terrace drinking beer in the middle of the afternoon while inside others are playing mahjong, slapping their ceramic tiles loudly on the glass table. The boss tells me that he has come to see how things are going at the office. When I ask about the potential for Chinese companies in this part of Laos his tone becomes curt and quite rude. 'You should ask what we are doing for these people,' he scoffs, and cranks his head towards the street outside. OK then. I ask him how he thinks Laos might benefit from Chinese investment in their rubber industry. 'Ha,' he tuts, and turns to leave the room. Over his shoulder he offers me his final piece of advice. 'If you want to know what we are doing for these people then why don't you ask them?'

Ruifeng has made an agreement with the Lao government to take 10,000 hectares of land for the development of a rubber plantation in the Long district of Luang Namtha province on a model called land concession. The exact fee paid by the company has never been disclosed, but they have publicly promised to invest in a water treatment plant and a new factory to bring jobs to the area.

The price of rubber in China is guaranteed by a price floor, which means the Chinese government ensures that Chinese farmers never get paid below a certain price for their crop. So as long as the prices in Laos are below this floor, then it is a very attractive source of rubber for processing companies like Ruifeng. To make Laos even more attractive, the Chinese government have added an extra incentive.

In the 1990s Laos was a major global supplier and exporter of opium. The golden triangle included most of Laos's northern territories and collectively it supplied nearly 40 per cent of the world's opium. Under significant international pressure, the Lao government tackled the issue first with a combination of eradication and crop replacement strategies and then, in a second wave of programmes, the Chinese and Laos governments offered companies generous tax breaks for investing in former opium-producing regions.

According to the terms agreed between the Chinese companies and the respective governments, a Chinese rubber company investing in northern Laos could lease land for 50 years and enjoy tax-free profits for the first seven years after harvesting began. They would be exempt from paying the land lease costs to the Lao government for the first nine years. They would also receive various benefits from the Chinese government, including interest-free loans. Furthermore, the Lao government guarantees freedom in cross-border movements of labour, equipment and vehicles, and exemption from tariff and import VAT. Under these terms, it is almost impossible for Chinese rubber companies not to look on Laos with wide eyes.

Laos's opium days are now firmly behind it – cultivation is restricted to isolated plots in remote villages and the country no longer supplies the international market (UNODC 2009). The Lao government declared Laos opium free as of 2006, with the United Nations Office on Drugs and Crime (UNODC)'s blessing. However, the opium replacement tax breaks continue. Ruifeng, for example, began investing in Laos long after it became 'opium free', but still will not pay any taxes on profits until seven years after production begins.

On the surface, it may sound like great news for the Laotians: huge investment from outside; the substitution of a legitimate trade in rubber for the morally questionable trade in opium. Moreover, China is pumping in huge sums of aid to its poorer neighbour. China is now the largest donor to an aid budget that funds 87 per cent of the Lao government's total expenditure, but given China's relative indifference to the welfare of its own people, I can't help wondering whether the Laotians are really getting such a good deal.

The engine of my Honda motorcycle screams in agony as I force it up yet another steep ravine, following closely in the tracks of Seeman's bike in front. It's an hour since we turned left off the main road where the Mekong river meanders along the Burmese border, and a day and a half since it started raining. The tracks we pass up and over have long since ceased to resemble anything that could be called a road. The impossible volume of water, mixed with the rich red Lao earth, has turned the paths into slippery chutes which we must slide down one side with care and scream up the other with open throttle.

On many occasions I have passed through places where farmers will predominantly favour a certain crop, which often gives the region its character – the vineyards of Southern France, the tulip fields of Kenya and the banana plantations of Central America all come to mind – but never before have I encountered such a monoculture as this. On both sides of this mountain, and as far as the eye can see, the mountains seen in every direction – north, south, east and west – are planted with one and only one crop: tall, slender trees with mottled silver bark trunks and heavy green foliage. Rubber.

We reach a particularly steep downward slope along the road, where the water has scarred the track so deeply that it resembles a freshly ploughed field. Seeman's motorbike's tyres cannot get a grip and, despite his best efforts to plant his feet, he skids out of control and falls sideways into the mud. He turns quickly to reassure me that he isn't seriously hurt and to warn me to be extra careful. His poncho is now covered in heavy red mud, but relentless rain will quickly wash it clean again in no time at all. Even had we swam across the Mekong, we could not be any wetter. There's something about rain like this that goes deeper than the clothes and the skin; it saturates your heart until it too feels heavy and sodden. I shudder under my poncho even though, despite the rain, the temperature is over 30 degrees and I carefully allow my bike to edge forward again, taking care not to follow the same route as Seeman.

Seeman is taking an enormous risk leading me to our destination, and I should say that Seeman is not his real name but the name he suggested I could safely use when I came to write about him. Laos is a totalitarian regime that strictly controls the flow of information from this northern region; several journalists have been denied permission to come here and so I have come on a tourist visa. But Seeman wants me to see what the Lao government do not want me to see, and evidently what the forces of nature aren't too keen on me seeing either.

Seeman and I stop at a junction in the track where a group of boys are collected under a makeshift shelter around a small smoky fire. The shelter is made from banana leaves and a ripped piece of plastic, and the water pours freely through in several places. The boys' clothes are soaked and they huddle close together for warmth. They laugh and joke with each other as I approach.

They explain to me that they have come here from the local villages in Long district. They usually work on their families' farms, but when the rainy season comes there is little for them to do, so they come up to the rubber plantations looking for work. This plantation, owned by the Chinese company Ruifeng, offers them work cleaning the undergrowth around the young rubber trees for $40 to $50 per week. The exact amount depends on how efficiently they work. 'I can get sixty dollars,' boasts one of the boys. 'Working for the Chinese is a good way to get money for us. But look.' He turns away, looking across the valley and the endless expanse of rubber plantation. 'There are no other trees. We understand the environmental impact. It is good and bad.'

Of course, before the arrival of rubber in northern Laos this land was all primary rainforest, full of biodiversity including one of the last populations of Asian forest elephants in existence. Such has been the haste to clear the land for rubber cultivation that below us a section of forest has been torched and the trees incinerated where they stood. Several of the scorched trunks are 3 or 4 metres in diameter. They will be bulldozed next week to finish them off. This kind of waste might seem illogical, but it is symptomatic of the pace at which the Lao government are determined to operate. This is deforestation as policy – the rainforest is expendable as long as the pursuit is development.

The Lao government and the rubber companies try to appease campaigners by claiming that they plant more rubber trees than they chop down old indigenous species. Laughably they claim that rubber companies are in fact engaged in 'reforestation' rather than 'deforestation'. One Chinese rubber company, Giti, even include this in their CSR material. But redefining rubber as a tree is misleading. Try explaining to an elephant or indeed an indigenous tribesman how they are meant to survive in a rubber forest.

Clearing weeds and scorched trees is hard work and there is danger too for the young men working in such an extreme environment with machines. If you have a contract with the company, they insure up to the first 1 million kip (around US$100). 'We do not have contracts,' the boys explain to me. Another man has a contract to clear the whole area so he gets the insurance, but he then outsources the work to these lads and many others like them, which means they are on their own if there is an accident. For these young men, it's a risk worth taking. At 19 years old they say they have nothing to lose and $40 is more than a little pocket money.

Further along the track, we stop at another shack by the road. Inside are two Chinese migrant workers from Yunnan. They too have come here to work in the plantations.

Ban Chagnee is a Lao village populated mostly by an indigenous people known in Laos as the Kui. Seeman has been here before, and after we have pulled the motorcycles off the road we head for a house in the centre of the village to shelter from the rain. The house belongs to a man named Borsai. Outside, his chickens run freely and in the back I can hear the distressed cries of a pig that is being tied up by his sons in preparation for becoming tonight's supper.

Borsai is in his mid-30s, squatting on his haunches as he pours three shots of a clear liquid from a glass bottle. With a wave of his hand he invites us to join him for an afternoon tipple of his home-made moonshine. After his 'loosener', he begins to talk freely, telling me about how life used to be in the village. 'The old way, we didn't have as much money but we had enough rice, we could raise a buffalo and more animals and we could get food from the forest. If we found cardamom in the forest then we could sell it for a little money.'

But life has changed for Borsai and the other villagers in Ban Chagnee with the arrival of the Chinese. 'Four years ago the [Lao] military arrived in the village and told us that the land on the mountain was being taken by the government and anyone who tried to grow rice there would be arrested.' For the Kui this was a disaster, as they have to rotate the fields where they grow rice or the land quickly runs out of the necessary nutrients. 'Now we need fertiliser so we can keep farming in one place, and it is expensive,' explains Borsai.

The problem was that, despite having farmed the land on the mountainside for generations, the Kui had no formal claim to it. Nobody in the village would be able to read the title document even if they did. The government's last five-year plan for 2006 to 2010 identified these regions as the hardest to develop due to high illiteracy rates and lack of access to markets for legal products. Here, a Kui person knows that a field is theirs by the rock that sits at the end of it or by the tree that casts a shadow on it. There are never land disputes within the village because it has always been so, and as far as the Kui were concerned no written document was ever necessary to formalise it.

The army paid some compensation to the villagers, but not for the land. 'Only for the work that we had done in the fields that they took. So if I had rice growing in that field, they paid me 2,000 kip ($0.25) for every day's work I had spent planting. No compensation for the rice, let alone for the land.' And it wasn't only the fields high up on the mountain that were taken. Some of the villagers' best land down in the valley was assigned on a three-year lease to the Chinese company for development into a nursery. New rubber saplings planted there could then be transferred higher up the mountain once they were ready. 'They were due to return that land last year but the company still haven't given it back. They say, "It is not up to us; talk to your government."'

The village also lost an important burial ground to the rubber plantation. For that they received just US$120. For the land where the company has built a factory and new houses for the Chinese technicians who run the business, US$30 was considered fair recompense. Borsai says they were told they could not appeal. I am beginning to understand why the government might not have wanted me to come here.

I have a feeling talking to Borsai that he and his fellow villagers are staring down the barrel of the twenty-first century. Whether they like it or not, change is coming and there's nothing they can do about it. The Lao government have chosen the path that they must now follow. In effect they have traded their land in exchange for jobs. 'We prefer the old way of life,' says Borsai. 'Yes, we can make money now, but our expenses are higher. We should spend money on rice but instead we spend it on things like motorbikes and phonecards and alcohol.' Having been so recently in Boten,

I can't help but feel it's only a matter of time before the casinos and prostitutes arrive and wonder how he will manage his money then.

The money that Borsai is talking about is the money he can earn working for Ruifeng, the Chinese company that bought the land on which he used to farm. Last year he and his wife signed up to clear 10 hectares of rubber plantation, which should have equated to 40 to 45 days' work. 'We nearly didn't finish in time last year, and so this year we are only doing seven hectares.' This speaks volumes about how these indigenous tribespeople feel about full-time work. There is a cultural gulf between the mindset of the indigenous tribesman who forages for enough food to feed his family and that required to perform the nine-to-five necessary to keep the wheels of the rubber plantation turning.

The stated aim of the Lao government in this is the reduction of poverty, but it is clear from talking to the Kui people that prior to the arrival of rubber they had little understanding of poverty or wealth. In effect they are being led by the nose into development and being proletariatised against their will by their new Chinese landlords.

Borsai says that the Chinese bosses are hard taskmasters. Often the work is closely supervised and workers taking breaks without good reason are fined: this rings remarkably true in light of what Zu had said about the Foxconn factory in China. Acceptable reasons include toilet and cigarette breaks. 'Many people who work for the company have taken up smoking,' claims Borsai. 'If you smoke then you can take more breaks.'

A freshly planted rubber plant takes seven years to reach maturity, when it can start to be tapped for latex to be turned into car tyres and running shoes. The Ruifeng plantation is nearing the point where tapping will soon begin, but it may take another five years to reach full capacity, with all of its 10,000 hectares being productive.

I am, of course, aware that there is a danger in the stance I find myself taking. Westerners tend to want change and material improvement for themselves but the status quo for everyone else, and when we see some of the disadvantages of a changing way of life – as is the case here in Laos – we are quick to condemn. The tourists coming to observe the tribespeople living the 'old ways' would happily have them preserved for all time, yet they are the first to demand the products that the intensive farming of rubber makes possible. We also have a tendency to ignore the fact that sometimes local people actually want the new way of life for the material benefits it may offer. And certainly, when it comes to the rubber industry in Laos, there are some who stand to gain from it.

Take Bounchang, for example. He is 15 years old and lives in a village near Ban Had Nyao. His typical day is pretty unrelenting: 'I usually wake up about three a.m. I get to this field for half past three because it is three kilometres from my house. There are 500 rubber trees in this field so I am cutting here for four or five hours. After I finish I come back to pick up the rubber and I get home at around one p.m. At home I help my family in the rice fields or cutting the weeds in the new tree area until four p.m. Every weekday I go to school for English from four-thirty until seven-thirty, and then I study computers from eight until ten p.m. After I get back home I warm a meal to eat and after I finish it is almost eleven o'clock so I go to bed. Often I get up and I think, "Ah, I haven't been asleep."' At this last thought, the young man chuckles to himself.

As he works from tree to tree in the darkness at 4 a.m.,

Bounchang lights his way with a torch strapped to the top of his head. He has a well-worked routine. First he empties last night's rainfall out of the empty bowl – made from half a coconut shell – tied to the side of the trunk, then he peels off any dried scum from the day before that might block the flow of fresh latex today. Finally, he takes the angled chisel in his right hand and begins to scrape a fresh channel into the bark, up and around the tree. Soon after, the white liquid rubber begins to seep into the groove and runs down through a metal spout that carries it clear of the trunk and into the empty bowl. Bounchang leaves the bowl to fill and moves on to the next tree.

His evenings, though, show that his work in the rubber plantation, while hard, is bringing him benefits. Apart from anything else, he can now afford the 5,000 kip per night that an English lesson in the community school costs him. Without the Ban Had Nyao rubber fields, Bounchang wouldn't be able to afford the education that he hopes will ultimately enable him to better himself and become a teacher.

There is, however, an important difference between Bounchang's life and that of the Kui people living in the forest. He does not work for a huge Chinese company. His own family have recently planted trees, though they will not start producing latex for another few years. At present he helps out on a farm owned by a local Lao farmer. Once the plants his father has sown are ready, he will already have the skills needed to run the new family business.

The farmer for whom Bounchang works is an impressive example of a Lao making his own way in this rapidly changing country. I meet this farmer, Han Yuang Sung, sitting on a stool outside his single-storey house in Ban Had Nyao. 'I was the first man in Laos to plant rubber,' he boasts. He smokes his cigarette right down to the butt and then starts to tear the filter to shreds while his wife, sitting next to him, silently crochets small yellow squares of fabric on to a piece of dark cloth. She never looks away but is all the while listening as her husband relays their common history. Han looks up again, forcing a smile with the few remaining teeth he has left, and continues. 'I worked for the NT government, but after the Vietnam War I fled to Thailand. Many Hmong people fled. We were scared that we would be arrested or worse.'

Although officially Laos remained neutral during the Vietnam War, the CIA recruited 60,000 Hmong hill tribesmen into a guerrilla army to fight the communists on the ground. When the war ended the communists ousted the NT government and the Hmong people fled over the border to refugee camps in Thailand. Han was one of tens of thousands who were offered repatriation to Europe, the United States or China. 'I didn't want to move too far away from my home and so I chose China,' says Han. 'When we got to China, I was given a job in a rubber-growing cooperative and I remained there for the next fourteen years.'

When Han's sons reached university age, they applied for places at Chinese universities. Despite having spent most of their lives in China, their applications were denied by the Chinese authorities on the grounds that they were not Chinese citizens. 'I felt hurt,' says Han. 'It was then that I looked to return to Laos.'

In the early 1990s, Laos was still a major player in terms of global opium production, with more than 30,000 hectares given over to cultivation. The problem was that while the government was committed to eradication and employed crop replacement strategies to encourage farmers to move to less socially damaging activities, farmers in the poorest areas didn't know what else to grow. Han applied to the district governor, a fellow Hmong, 16 years after he had left Laos, with a plan to plant rubber. He received a grant under the poppy eradication scheme to move to Luang Namtha with his family.

'I picked Luang Namtha because the people here are my people, Hmong. But also because the geography is very similar to southern China. I knew that I could grow rubber here the same way that I had learned to there.' Rubber is not an easy crop to grow. It must be planted and then coaxed and then grafted and then finally transplanted. It is a delicate process that needs to be learned. Then, when it is grown, it must be tapped carefully to ensure constant supply. These were skills that had been passed down for generations in China, but now they had fallen into Lao hands.

'Nobody in this village knew about rubber when I first came here.' Han dedicated every hectare he could to planting rubber and planted only enough rice to feed his family. 'Of course people were suspicious of me. They didn't understand rubber, but they watched me very carefully. Eventually, when we started to harvest the latex and export it for money, the same people came to me to ask if I could help them.'

Han and his sons now collectively have 20 hectares of rubber and 1,700 trees are already producing 20 tonnes of latex per annum, which at current prices of 10 yuan per kilo means they bring in a very good income of 200,000 yuan (£20,000). In return for bringing the skills with him, Han received the land from the community. Now in Ban Had Nyao every family grows rubber. The village has a contract with a Chinese importer but they are free to negotiate with anyone they choose. 'I'm not rich,' says Han. 'Somewhere in the middle. Let's say we have enough.'

The village is not a cooperative. Farmers manage their own land and are free to grow and sell whatever they please. However, every farmer has gradually been won over to the benefits of growing rubber. Ban Had Nyao farmers have also found that together they have greater bargaining power with the Chinese importers. Together they are harder to exploit and so the price they get is good. They have even seen an opportunity to get a better price still.

The Ban Had Nyao farmers are building their own primary processing plant. Rubber goes through several processing stages and the village hopes to be able to perform the first stage right here. 'The value of our exports would go up to twenty-five yuan per kilo.' Han smiles at the prospect. Not everyone has been able to contribute the same amount to the building, so the plan is to recoup the costs first, after which everyone in Ban Had Nyao can begin to benefit.

And this is the point. We in the developed world might bemoan the loss of traditional farming and the rise of rubber plantations, but at least people like Han are masters of their own fate. Han has taken charge of his own development, working for the local community as well as himself. 'I worry about all the Chinese companies coming into Laos,' says Han. 'How will they find enough people to work all those trees?' A rubber plantation requires five to ten people per hectare to maintain it once it is in full production. Add up all the land ceded to Chinese companies already and that means over 1 million people are going to be needed. 'Are they planning to bring a million Chinese here to Laos?' asks Han. 'What will that do to our culture?'

Currently, China brings a different kind of investment package to the table from that offered by Western states – one that does not carry conditions that insist on compliance with human rights, democratic ideals and environmental protection. Instead China builds relationships with foreign governments through the construction of important cultural and state buildings, such as the National Stadium in Laos – 'gifts of friendship' that are designed to build relationships. The real challenge for developing nations like Laos is how to take the aid and foreign investment on which they are so dependent with one hand and yet have enough strength in the other to enforce regulations to ensure that Chinese companies don't bypass local regulations or exploit their own people in ways that would even be in violation of the laws of China.

At least 150,000 hectares of land has already been ceded to Chinese investors for 30 to 50 years at knockdown prices with overgenerous tax breaks. The Lao government is so desperate to further its own development that it is in danger of selling itself off on the cheap. Land conflicts with villagers are on the rise as plantations encroach on village fields and nearby forests, taking away traditional livelihoods with little or no compensation. This may very well be the cost of progress, but what is the return?

Aside from the environmental and social impacts of such investments, what benefits do the Lao people accrue from this development? Jobs and disposable income for the workers is the claim made by the government. Is this what the villagers said they wanted? A steady job with a steady salary? And what guarantees are there that a Chinese migrant worker with more experience, a stronger work ethic and who speaks the same language as the boss won't take that job away?

The other danger for Laos is that Chinese investors will want to see a quick return on their investments and that the current agreements already provide for free movement of labour from China. So if the companies deem it necessary, and in all likelihood ethnic Lao villagers will not be able to adjust to the culture shock of working for a Chinese company quickly enough, the result could be an influx of Chinese immigrants to get the job done.

Like so many countries around the world taking money from China, all Laos has to sell to its large northern neighbour are its commodities. What they buy in return is mostly Chinese technology, machinery and consumer goods, many of which are of low quality, but within reach of poorer consumers there. Informal (or illegal) trade in commodities is widespread in the three Mekong countries: Laos, Cambodia and Vietnam. For instance, state officials in Vietnam estimate that the majority of the coal and rubber exported to China is informal, with no duties paid to the state and no records of exact exported tonnage and value.

China is by no means the only country not playing by the rules. Campaigners from NGOs in the area cite similar disregard for ethical considerations from companies from Malaysia, South Korea and Russia, but Chinese investment is by far the largest. China's demand for natural rubber is estimated to reach 11.5 million tonnes per annum by 2020, about 30 per cent of the world's total production as China's growing demand for transport reaches 200 million vehicles.

Furthermore, Chinese investment is two-pronged: private investment, which is soaring, and state investment, which has an almost inexhaustible pot of cash to spend. And Laos is not the only country with whom China has dealings in this way. I have focused on Laos and the trade in rubber, but I could just as easily have talked about fishing rights in Western Africa and Latin America or copper mining in Peru and Afghanistan. As China has built up huge dollar reserves from its export boom, it is increasingly looking to invest them in overseas natural resources. Since 2004, when China announced its Going Global Strategy, the intention has been to meet regional shortages for natural resources by looking globally. Thus, this new investment strategy led by the state has subsidised Chinese companies to go boldly in search of the materials needed to sustain the boom.

Chinese politicians have been reluctant to enforce greater social responsibility, either internally on their own investment policy or externally through legislation imposed on private companies. Chinese officials often claim that it is too early in China's development to make such ethical considerations a priority – ethics are a luxury only affordable by rich Western countries. We have already enjoyed the spoils of our own empires, so why shouldn't China build its own? It looks as though the human cost of nineteenth-century empire-building is about to repeat itself.

But China cannot be held solely accountable for this. Major companies in the developed world are complicit. Just as they have a tendency to turn a blind eye to the conditions in which manufactured goods are produced in China, so they rarely question just how the raw materials are produced. The supply chain for rubber is difficult for a casual observer to trace as it goes through several processes before it becomes a car tyre or a training shoe. But Western manufacturers can and should track back to the source.

When it is in their economic interests, Western companies are quick to do this kind of tracking. Rubber in particular is a heavy material and so consequently is expensive to transport. No surprise then that the world's largest tyre manufacturer, Bridgestone, has recently built a processing factory just over the border in Meng La. Publicly Bridgestone have a strong position on social responsibility: 'Bridgestone is more than just a corporation. We're a part of society, and believe we have an important role to play in improving life for everyone' (www.bridgestone.com 2010). Let's hope that 'everyone' includes the people of northern Laos.

What I'd seen in Laos made me realise the difficulty for ethical consumers of tracing the credentials of their favourite products. What is more, Laos is at least a relatively stable country. I began to wonder how much worse it could be if the raw materials were coming from one of the regions of the world where conflict reigns. I decided that to see for myself I would have to travel further, to one of capitalism's most perilous front lines.

5

A mine of disinformation

Congo: South Kivu

'How would they eat if I did not buy their minerals?'

Kika and I are crouched down at the entrance to the Congolese mine. Inside Boniface is looking back towards us and the other miners. Everyone seems to have stopped work and Kika is clearly excited to have me here and enjoying being the centre of attention. He wants me to go inside the mine and urges me to move forward with a hurried shake of his hand. He chatters constantly. 'A group of ten can easily get ten tonnes. Twenty tonnes even. Using your hammers to break off the stones. When you find a big stone you do this . . .' He begins to jump up and down, miming a hammering motion with his hammer and pick. 'Then everybody is happy.'

I agree just to 'stick my head in' for a sense of the space inside. I have to bend low to get under the beam supporting the entrance and then it is easier to crouch on my haunches and shuffle inside. Kika follows me, and Boniface immediately turns and scampers a little farther along. 'Go after him,' says Kika, motioning with his torch. The mine ahead is dark, a little over waist-level in height and cramped. I am soon aware that my breath is a lot heavier than it was outside. Staying crouched down as low as I can manage, I waddle from foot to foot using my hands to steady myself until I feel that I am fully inside the mine. Looking back, I'm surprised how the light from the entrance already looks small. Looking the other way, everything is pitch black.

Unsure what to do next, I let out a heavy sigh which makes Kika laugh. The ceiling becomes so low that even now, crouching down as far as I can, my head dislodges some dirt from the ceiling above. It is also much narrower than it was at the entrance and there isn't enough room to move my arms. Our torches give out only a dim light, enough to see the way but not enough to see any real distance ahead. I reach into my zip pocket and take out a little point-and-shoot camera. In the darkness, it beeps as I hold down the button and then the flash lights up the tunnel for an instant. I turn it over to check the display and I suddenly get a clearer digitally enhanced picture of where we are.

The floor of the tunnel is a soft pillow of fine, dark brown dirt, but the walls are fiery shades of red and orange rock. All along the tunnel, every three or four feet apart, there are wooden supports roughly fashioned from tree trunks and branches – two simple vertical posts to the side with a horizontal beam spanning to give support to the ceiling. The wood is bent and misshapen, flaking a little from the damp air in the shaft. The camera has picked out Boniface crouched down in the dirt looking back towards me. Beyond him the flash can only pick out another four supports, which I estimate is around 15 feet.

'I'm not going all the way down there,' I say to Kika. He laughs again. I realise that I'm laughing too as a way of dealing with the fear. I'm not entirely sure why he's laughing; maybe it's all just a little surreal for him to see a *muzungu* in a mine shaft. I don't know. But I feel compelled to go further.

'Conor, where are you?' I recognise the voice of Amani, my translator. He said he wasn't going to come but the others at the entrance to the mine have pressurised him into checking that I am

OK. They have made him feel so bad for not coming with me that he has come far underground, and I can tell from the shake in his voice that he doesn't feel safe. I push on another 20 metres to where the shaft seems suddenly to bend sharply to the right. 'I think that's far enough,' I say again. It seems to just go on and on for miles. Kika catches up with me as I take another picture. This time the camera's display tells me nothing. It has been useful up until now, but it can't see around corners. 'Do you want to go further?' he asks. I can tell he wants me to see more. He shouts something in Swahili back to Amani and, whatever it was, it persuades Amani to come further. He says, 'It's not far now, just the other side.'

'OK. Let's see,' I say, resigned to my fate.

'Do I come with you?' Amani's voice now sounds like that of a frightened child.

'If you like,' I tell him.

He catches up with my shoulder just as I begin to shift back on to all fours and stops me with a hand. 'Conor, I am afraid.'

'I'm afraid too, Amani.'

I'm laughing again. Of course I'm afraid. I actually hear myself say out loud, 'I'm going to die writing this fucking book.' I've since played these words back on my Dictaphone, which was recording the whole time, listening to the fear in my own voice and trying to find in it, and so in myself, the reason for continuing down that dark, cramped, treacherous tunnel after Boniface's dim torchlight. A feeling is what I believe I was chasing, a need to feel, if only for a few moments, what these men, like Boniface scrambling along in front of me, probably used to and certainly should feel but probably no longer do every time they risk their lives to go far under this earth, into this sweaty, dirty death chamber in pursuit of a living.

I simply have to see the face of this mine. I've come this far. How can I understand what these men do every day if I cannot see it even once? I'm laughing, but that is only a device for self-preservation. In fact I'm blocking out the fear to push myself on. Now I'm crawling on my hands and knees, as the tunnel has become so low and narrow that I can barely squeeze through it at all. Amani's fear (or sense perhaps) gets the better of him and he stops. I continue following the dim light of Boniface's torch. I am panting heavily and the air now feels heavy and wet. I stop again. This is crazy. I shout back up the tunnel to see how far I am from where Amani stopped: at least another 20 metres. Kika is coming too – right behind me. 'It's another twenty metres,' he says. He is panting a little now too. 'Oh fuck it. Let's do it,' I hear myself say. I seem to have switched off the part of my brain that stops me being stupid. I'm not going to stop again until I catch up with Boniface. Head down, scramble on and then suddenly, he's there. I can see it.

Boniface is squatted down in a pool of muddy water. Around him is the face of the mine. A vault of stone coloured in the most incredible stripes of reds and yellows and oranges like the inside of a giant candy wrapper. He takes the point of his pick and directs my eye to a seam of dark black stone running vertically from ceiling to floor. 'Cassiterite,' he says, smiling and nodding. He turns back to it and starts to hammer his pick into the rock, displacing pieces of it into the dirty pool. He holds his body still and swings his arm down to hammer hard on the pick and then he lifts slightly to adjust his position and swings hard again.

Suddenly I feel another rush of fear. The sight of rock coming away from the walls is particularly unsettling. I want to get out of here. The crashing noise of the hammer on the pick is beginning to make me feel dizzy and uncomfortable. For these men this is exactly the fear that they must become desensitised to. They have to put their own fear of death to one side to come to this place every day of their lives. They know the risks better than anyone, but for them there is no choice. Life is such that the only living to be made is found here, deep within the bowels of the jungle where violent storms can blow in without warning creating enough water in minutes to trigger landslides that can bury them alive. I take another picture of Boniface chipping away at the rock in the dim light – I don't want to forget a single detail – and then I turn and begin to scramble back.

Safely back outside, I am panting heavily and covered in dirt. As I crawled back up through the tunnel, an important question occurred to me that I hadn't even considered before. What knowledge do these men have of what happens to the minerals after they sell them? How much knowledge do they have of their vital importance to the supply chain of the electronic goods that drive the global economy? 'We do not know what these minerals are used for,' laughs Kika. 'We only know that you use them in your country.' He repeats the question in Swahili to his friends to see if they have any thoughts. Jean Claude checks with his pals before he offers me an answer. 'We heard that coltan is used for Motorola cell phones but we do not know if this is true. Maybe cassiterite is used to make padlocks or cooking pots.' The rest of the crowd all turn at once and look to me to see if Jean Claude is right.

We begin to make our way back through the jungle, filing along the edge of a huge pit of thick, wet, heavy orange clay. Down below a muscular young man in only a pair of white nylon running shorts digs the earth away while his companion turns his head up to look at me. He explains to Kika that the rain in the night has caused a landslide and the entrance to the mineshaft has been buried beneath.

I have met former miners in the UK who talk of missing the camaraderie down the mine. Kika is no different. 'Friendship in the mine is better than friendship in the village or even in your family.' We pause to take stock of how best to cross a swampy stretch of ground before he continues, 'Sometimes if the mine collapses on you and covers you, your friend in the mine will not run away; they will stay and try to look for you.' But despite this bond, sometimes there's nothing you can do with only picks and shovels. 'Sometimes it is hard to even find the body of the dead because it is so buried under heavy stones. I have seen it several times. I have already lost several of my friends, my life companions.'

Fortunately nobody is missing today, but the men have been digging all morning to uncover the entrance so that they can begin work inside it again. The equipment the miners are using seems so basic that it strikes me as nothing short of miraculous that they would know where in the dense jungle to find valuable minerals. This is the sort of terrain that geological surveyors spend months working on for mineral companies. 'This is a mine where the Belgians were mining,' says Kika. 'It has not been worked since Independence in 1960. We began digging here again two years ago for cassiterite.'

One of these men is older than the other boys – in fact, he tells me he is nearly 50. 'This is my job. I grew up mining,' he tells me. It has funded his family of ten children. 'I remember what the mines were like soon after the Belgians left. I used to come to the mine when my father worked underground. The Belgians built rails so that we could pull the minerals out easily. But now we must pass them hand to hand in a chain. It is much more dangerous.

And when the Belgians were here we always had generators to pump out the water in the mine. It is the water that causes the landslides. It is much more dangerous in the mines than when the Belgian equipment still worked.'

During the past 50 years, while the rest of the world has made giant leaps forward, first in manufacturing and then in technology and communications, here at the heart of Africa things have gone steadily backwards. Even colonial Belgian miners of the 1950s were able to dig with greater safety than today's twenty-first-century Congolese. The lack of any health and safety regulation is a symptom of the lack of large Western mining companies in the area. Big Western-run mines bring health and safety procedures as well as steady wages and often housing too. But the Western companies are being encouraged to stay away by both the good guys and the bad.

This is a far cry from what is happening in Laos, and not just because of the way the raw materials are being sourced. Laos is by no means a utopian dream but compared to the Democratic Republic of Congo (DRC) it has a lot going for it – it is at least politically stable and at peace. Congo, on the other hand, strikes me as a complete basket case. Nowhere is safe. The miners run huge risks underground, and things don't improve much when they get back to the surface. Back in Kika's village the burnt remains of several houses lie next to newly built ones. Kika comes over to where I am standing looking down at the scorched earth. 'We are fresh from war and we are still at war,' he tells me. 'People worried here because their homes were completely put down on fire by FDLR. People were running there in the jungle to hide themselves.' His finger is tracing an arc around the thick forest in front of us.

'Our homes were destroyed, our precious valuable things destroyed. Our women were raped and our cows were looted. And they are here still. FDLR are in the thickest jungles and they are in the mines too. They know the paths better even than the Congolese army. The Congolese soldiers have no chance against them in this jungle.' But for now, we both know that they're the best he's got. We both look down at the blackened ground where Kika's wellington boot rolls back and forth distractedly over a piece of blackened mud brick. He kicks it away and we stand silently together.

Historically, Congo has been no stranger to human misery. Its current problems started with the Rwandan genocide in 1994 when 900,000 Tutsis were murdered in a little over 100 days. The Hutu leaders who took power failed to hold on to it for long and the Tutsis quickly regained control. Hutus, fearing reprisal for their abominable acts, fled in the tens of thousands, over the border to refugee camps in eastern Congo.

The following year, a young Congolese soldier, Laurent Kabila, seeking to overthrow the unpopular despot President Mobutu Sese Seko, gathered an army in eastern Congo. He received help from Uganda and Rwanda and in October 1996 the joint armies marched over the border in the name of liberating the Congolese people. Unfortunately the Rwandan forces had another agenda – to exact revenge on the Hutus hiding out in Congo. As they moved west through eastern Congo, the joint Kabila/Rwandan army began attacking the refugee camps and slaughtering thousands of Hutu men, women and children. People in the camps had no choice but to flee into the Congolese jungle to hide. Eventually they regrouped and founded their own armed force – the FDLR (Democratic Forces for the Liberation of Rwanda, or *Forces démocratiques de libération du Rwanda*).

By the time 'Africa's World War' ended in 2003, an estimated

5 million people had perished. Congo's neighbours agreed to withdraw their armies but the FDLR were left behind. Still determined to return one day to 'liberate' Rwanda, they continued to bide their time in Congo's jungles. The FDLR, an army without a state, perpetrated innumerable atrocities against the civilian population during this time. Rape in particular became the new instrument of war and tens of thousands of eastern Congolese women and girls were systematically kidnapped, raped and mutilated to instil fear into the hearts of rural communities.

The existence of FDLR in Congo's jungles has often provided justification for the formation of independent armed groups claiming to defend the citizens of Congo. The most recent of these is the National Congress for the Defence of the People, or *Congrès national pour la défense du peuple* (CNDP). Like most of these groups, the CNDP have established themselves through the use of extreme violence and terror. Like those before them, they have been rewarded with senior military and political positions as well as valuable mineral-rich territory put under their control. The result is a national army populated by individuals accused of perpetrating some of the worst atrocities against civilians. When in 2009 the CNDP became the latest of these groups to be integrated into the Congolese army, it was rewarded with control of much of South Kivu. This system of impunity has resulted in a grotesque culture of reward for rape and murder.

Some sense of the lawlessness and brutality of Congo is apparent when I visit a small United Nations-run base designated for debriefing former FDLR combatants in Goma. Standing on the shore of Lake Kivu, in a small tented section of the UN base opposite the dilapidated ruins of what was once President Mobutu's summer house, is the area now designated for debriefing former FDLR combatants who have either been captured or given themselves up. A joint UN and Rwandan government initiative aims to repatriate the soldiers to Rwanda and offer them retraining, houses and jobs.

Statistics produced by the UN mission in Congo (MONUC) suggest that in 2009 over 1,500 combatants and their families were sent back. That should mean 1,500 fewer potential killers in the jungles of Congo but unfortunately the traffic runs both ways. The riches on offer in the Congolese jungles mean that many more young Rwandan men are still being enticed to travel to Congo to join the FDLR and profit from the trade in minerals.

The tents are arranged in rows like a soldiers' mess, which could easily be taken for a military camp were it not for the dresses and children's clothes hanging up to dry along the rolls of razor wire that form the perimeter. The security is more for those inside than out – if the local Congolese people knew they were here, there is no doubt they would happily lynch every last one of them.

Safina has taken this *nom de guerre* since he joined the FDLR 14 years ago when he was 17. Now he's relaxing on his bed opposite me in a pair of green flip-flops that match his FC Barcelona football shirt but clash rather dramatically with his plaid golf trousers. He has a baseball cap pulled down tight on to his round head. His eyes are pitch dark and he has a small moustache, out of which emerges a deep pronounced scar that runs right up the length of his broad nose. Given the reputation of FDLR combatants as rapists and murderers of civilians, it feels strangely intimate to be sitting like this, like two soldiers in the mess, having a casual chat.

We talk over the loud hum of the camp generator running outside the tent and the crackling, spitting sound of meat being fried in oil outside. The smell of the meat mixed with burning firewood wafts through the tent as Safina begins to describe to me how he joined the FDLR soon after the Rwandan genocide. 'I joined FDLR to avenge the murder of my parents and to liberate Rwanda from their killers. But now I must think to put my family first.' Safina's wife was recently captured and deported to Rwanda. So he has made the decision to put down his arms and return with his children to join her there. 'I will make a new life there,' he says. 'In Rwanda, I will be a businessman.'

The FDLR gave Safina an education beyond how to kill. 'Within the camp,' he explains, 'we were schooled in many things: military strategy, logistics, even international human rights, but we had also to be self-sustaining.' Nobody can be sure exactly how many FDLR are still active in the Democratic Republic of Congo, but estimates range from 6,000 to 12,000 combatants. These men have to be continually armed, housed and fed and that requires money. As an army without a state, they have no financial support from outside; all their funds need to be self-generated from within DRC. As such, the FDLR must be run like a business and Safina and his fellow officers act as the line managers.

'If I would send a group of my soldiers into the villages then they must come back with some benefit for the company. If not then they would be punished.' It doesn't take much imagination to see how a group of young men, armed with AK-47s, sent to a remote area of the jungle with those instructions, made their living. The FDLR have established a feudal hold in the remote communities where people are making ready cash from mining, leeching a profit from them and using terror, murder, violence and rape as their unique selling point.

In the jungles, the FDLR have established themselves as part of the fabric of Congo. They exist to make money and they remain because they are successful at it. FDLR soldiers often take Congolese wives who can pass easily into the markets in town to offload the minerals plundered by their husbands and return with much-needed goods and food in exchange. Like Safina, they see themselves as traders, making money as legitimately as the Congolese soldiers against whom they are nominally at war. And the longer this status quo exists, and as long as there is a market for their 'goods' in the West, then the more normal it seems to the men in their ranks.

Safina was responsible for 95 soldiers. He seems very aware of his surroundings now in a United Nations camp. 'No, I didn't give orders to loot or murder civilians, but of course . . .' He holds out his open hands as if to affirm his innocence. '. . . Some young soldiers would do these things . . .' His voice trails off and his gaze drifts with it into the distance as though he is remembering something that he doesn't want to talk about. 'Even if you had killed civilians,' he continues, now looking down towards his feet, 'when you were repatriated to Rwanda, the international community would find you and punish you for these things.' He learned enough human rights in the jungle, it seems, to know not to say any more.

I ask him whether he now feels any remorse or guilt for things he has done during his time with the FDLR. A smile returns to his face and he shakes his head. 'No. Not at all.' It strikes me that one of the cruellest dimensions of this ten-year war is the complete absence of funding for many of the forces fighting in it. Armies left to support themselves in an area rich with gold and coltan and cassiterite will of course exploit them to generate revenue. Hungry soldiers will steal from those who have food. They don't need to go down the mines themselves, only operate in areas where others do and then plunder the spoils when they can.

*

The appalling, almost casual violence of everyday existence goes a long way to explain why boys like Kika and the other miners are prepared to risk their lives digging cassiterite out of the ground. Yes, he may well die in a landslide, but then he might equally perish in a night raid when the FDLR come looking for the spoils. 'You feel afraid, but since it is the only way of getting money you cannot do otherwise.' He seems so calm as he talks that it makes me feel even more uneasy. 'You have to go back. If you are unlucky you die there. If you are lucky you get money to do your life.'

Kika has made the calculations. Life here isn't just cheap, it is free. That being so, he reckons, you might as well risk dying for something rather than face the likelihood of dying for nothing. Perhaps sensing my unease, Kika stops and turns to face me. 'We like being miners. To be a miner you must be strong and well fed.' He flexes his biceps like a body builder and flashes me a reassuring smile. 'It is a good job.'

As well as Amani, Kika and his friend, we have three CNDP soldiers accompanying us on this particular expedition. This area is now under the control of the official Congolese army, the FRDC. The recent deal has brought their former enemy, the CNDP, into the fold so that they are now, at least nominally, part of the same side. For Kika and the other miners, it means protection from the FDLR, but at a cost. The reality for artisanal miners here is that there is always someone to be paid: if it's not the FDLR then it's someone else. The CNDP colonel who controls this area charges the miners a tax on all the cassiterite that they bring up from the mines. This is officially 'illegal', but who can Kika complain to?

This may all seem a very long way from the interests and concerns of Western consumers. And it would be were it not for the raw material that Kika and his colleagues are risking their lives for. Cassiterite is one of those products that few have heard of, yet it is something most of us use every day. It provides the tin that holds together the circuit boards of our mobile phones, laptops and countless other electronic products. It is found in any quantity in only a small number of countries, and of these Congo is by far Africa's largest producer. Indeed it is the fifth largest producer of cassiterite in the world. The multibillion-dollar global electronics trade would be virtually unthinkable without it.

And that poses an ethical dilemma. We need cassiterite, but should we trade with a country whose human rights record is so utterly appalling? The UN thinks not. The UN has repeatedly supported calls for a ban on the trade in DRC's minerals. That's fine in principle, but when a country has something everyone else wants there is always a way to sidestep the official line. Since I arrived in Congo people have kept mentioning one name to me, the name of a mineral exporter who was cited in a recent UN report as being one of those at the centre of the trade in conflict minerals. If I want to know more about how the trade really works, I have been told, then I must go to Bukavu, a town in the east of the country, and talk to him. I must talk to Panju.

Bukavu, it has to be said, looks best from a distance. You need to look at the town from more than, say, 100 yards. That way you can't see the deep ravines in the mud roads, the dilapidation of the buildings or the filth on the streets, but rather you can take in the 'big picture' – a city of some half a million people built into the picturesque hillsides of five peninsulas that jut out into the tranquil Lake Kivu. From a distance, those dilapidated old colonial buildings have a certain decadence – a style and charm even. A few large new modern houses are beginning to spring up too as wealthy Congolese buy the best remaining prime real estate spots.

It suggests a new source of wealth, but in truth the source is the same – eastern Congo's mineral mines. Only the people making the money from them have changed.

Bukavu is a product of war, a town of crime, filth and decay; a town so poor that when they are going downhill the taxi drivers turn off their engines to save fuel. The roads are so pocked with potholes that cars constantly have to navigate around them. 'Which side of the road are you supposed to drive on in this town?' I ask one taxi driver. 'The side with the least potholes,' he replies. In the outskirts the roads are simply mud lanes running through mud brick and corrugated-iron-roofed shanties. When it rains, which it does most days, it comes down so hard that the roads become dangerous to walk on. At night those same roads are dangerous for a whole other set of more sinister reasons. Bukavu draws few tourists. Several NGOs have become long-term residents of the town, providing the occasional glimpse of a foreign face, but otherwise Bukavu is pure Congo.

The sales house or *comptoir* is a heavily fortified, two-storey grey concrete building with a wide gate lined with rolls of razor wire. I try to peek through to see what is going on inside, but there's not even a crack of light to be seen. Whoever owns this place clearly doesn't want anyone to see what's going on inside.

Above the main door is a clue to the owner's identity. Written simply in bold white type is the word 'Panju'. I knock loudly on the door and a short, squat and vaguely threatening-looking man appears and asks in Swahili what we want. I explain that I want to talk to his boss about buying some minerals. There's a suspicion of Westerners now among the sales houses that act as middlemen for Congo's minerals since the UN accused them of directly funding the FDLR. Panju was specifically named in the report.

[The UN] calculates that FDLR earn . . . a few million dollars a year from this [cassiterite] trade. The Group also established that MDM, World Mining Company (WMC), Etablissment Muyeye and Panju, mineral-exporting businesses for knowingly purchasing minerals from FDLR-controlled areas, have continued throughout 2009 to trade in minerals originating from some of the same FDLR-controlled areas. (United Nations)

To get around this, I have decided to pass myself off as a potential investor or at least an adviser to a potential investor. I tell the man in a firm voice to get his boss, firm enough to sound like I mean business but careful not to piss him off. He's still being fairly threatening. He tells me to wait and slams the door shut.

Amani and I wait. The street outside is setting up for market. On both sides of the traffic, women and children are laying out their wares for sale on blankets thrown out on to the mud floor – today's bargains include a mix of nuts and avocados, T-shirts and textiles.

The door opens and a taller man with a full head of white hair and a very prominent bulbous nose appears, dressed in a smart Ralph Lauren yellow checked shirt and a pair of slacks. He is clearly not Congolese but his origin is difficult to place from his accent as he greets me with a circumspect '*Bonjour*'. The same is apparently not true of me because when I reply in French he switches to English: 'Come in.'

I follow Panju into a long cool corridor towards his office and suddenly begin to feel a little anxious. I can feel my heart racing. I need to really keep myself together if I am going to pull off this deceit. It irks me that this is necessary, but necessary it is, because as we sit down either side of his large desk Panju leans across to me and asks me straight out, 'You're not a journalist, are you? I don't talk to journalists.'

The threatening-looking man who first opened the door to us is still waiting in the doorway, his arms folded across his chest. Other than the desk there is little else in the room. One lonely looking bookshelf has a couple of mining directories and a French–Chinese dictionary. Panju is waiting for his answer. No, I explain to him. I am an economist. It is my job to research various industries across the developing world, not just mining. For example, I have just conducted a study of the coffee industry in Tanzania.

I explain that I have strong links with various investment companies in the UK to whom I frequently feed back the results of my research and that these may be particularly relevant to his own business interests. Most of this is actually close enough to the truth that I feel as though I'm talking pretty confidently and fluently. Panju turns to the man in the doorway and with a flick of his head ushers him away – I've done enough to convince him. The heavy is no longer required.

I explain to Panju that my investors are sure that there are fundamentally profitable opportunities for them in Congo, but that the Western investment environment is increasingly being influenced by ethical considerations so it is no longer acceptable to explore any opportunity without considering the ethical dimensions. In particular many people are concerned about the recent UN report.

Panju wastes no time in sharing his view of the UN report – 'Total bullshit'. One of the fundamental claims of the report was that the mineral trade in Congo was directly funding the activities of the FDLR. 'It is just wrong to say that we are buying minerals from rebels,' he says. 'Just look outside where we are buying minerals and you won't see any rebels.' Of course, he may not be buying directly from the rebels, but there's no saying whether the minerals may have passed through rebel hands somewhere along the supply chain, as there are so many middlemen involved. 'Yes, that is true for sure. But what are we to do? We are not fighters; we are businessmen. We do not deal with rebels but the UN did not come here to see for themselves how we are conducting our business or who we are buying our minerals from.'

Panju leads me down a maze of corridors to a courtyard outside, where 30 or so young men sit in the shady patches around the edge where the high walls hide them from the afternoon sun. They are mostly small-time middlemen and miners preparing their minerals for sale. Some are unpacking dark stones from hessian sacks; others are working in pairs pounding and smashing the rocks in metal tins and then sifting through to separate out the pure dust. Almost all of the men have brought cassiterite to sell, transported here in the boots of cars or on the back of trucks from the remote areas of the jungle where the mines are.

'You see, it is hard work,' Panju points out. 'And what do the UN want them to do instead? How would they eat if I did not buy their minerals? Who is going to pay them, if not me?' This question is clearly meant to be rhetorical, as Panju continues to walk towards a large storeroom at the far end of the courtyard. 'And there were many more before the report.'

Just inside the storeroom is a large wooden board with a warning written across the top to all those coming to sell minerals. It is a list of areas that the UN has declared 'no buy' zones. 'We can't buy minerals from these areas.' Panju begins to read the areas on the list: 'Lulingu, Casese, Lemera and Mwenga.' Having just returned from two of these areas and seen cassiterite being mined with my own eyes, this is a little surprising. The UN report recommends that companies like Panju's should never simply accept verbal assurances from their suppliers regarding the origin of minerals without 'credible supporting documentation'.

'But how can you tell which region the minerals are really coming from when there is clearly no documentation?' I ask, looking around the room at 20 identical glistening black piles of minerals, which have been delivered in the boots of cars from goodness knows where. He pauses, looking for the right expression. 'Good luck?' I offer. He chuckles, perhaps appreciative that someone understands his problem, and pats me on the back. 'Thank you. Yes, exactly. Good luck,' he repeats.

The UN report has hit his business hard, yet he is clearly still trading and the overall exploitation of Congolese minerals shows no sign of slowing down. The mines in all areas, including those controlled by the FDLR, are still churning out gold, coltan (another mineral required for the production of mobile phones) and cassiterite destined ultimately for use in products sold in Asia and the West, but the result of the ethical embargo encouraged by the UN is simply to create a black market for them. Panju estimates that the volume of coltan and cassiterite going through Bukavu sale houses is down around 50 tonnes per month but not because it isn't being mined. DRC is still exporting its minerals, just not legally.

In the course of our conversation, the names of Panju's major customers start to emerge. One is Malaysia. The Malaysian Smelting Corporation (MSC) is the world's third largest supplier of smelted metals. It is also the biggest buyer of cassiterite from Congo and neighbouring Rwanda. Officially, the *comptoirs* are legitimate, which allows their customers, such as MSC, to claim that their supply chains are clean and legal.

Panju's other key customer is, not surprisingly, China. 'My European buyers have all stopped buying from DRC now and

Thailand [Thaisarco] too now is talking about stopping,' he informs me. 'Only my customers in Malaysia and China are still buying.' He laughs. 'It is different with them. The Chinese care mostly about the price.'

Panju calls over his nephew, who runs to the office to fetch a printout of an email. It is from Panju's Chinese customer, written in fairly bad English but with a clear enough meaning. After thanking Panju for the recent shipment of 15 tonnes of coltan, the buyer goes on to say that he would like to place a further order. Fairly standard stuff, but then it goes on to request something quite irregular. The email asks that the paperwork for the next shipment be altered to disguise that the minerals are from Congo: 'Please change country of origin documentation so that Ethiopia or Rwanda is country of origin.'

The UN budget for operations in Congo is over $100 million per month. Panju believes that this is motivation for the United Nations to make the situation in DRC seem worse than it is. He has another solution to the war against the FDLR. 'Let the UN divide that money between FDLR,' suggests Panju. 'They say there are 8,000 FDLR soldiers active in eastern Congo. Share out one month's worth of the UN money between them. Offer them each 12,500 dollars to put down their guns and go back to Rwanda. They wouldn't hesitate. They would all go straight away. Problem solved.'

Panju makes another, very telling, point. 'The ethics of the West are now incompatible with those of the Third World. In my opinion, in twenty years the West will have no more business interests in the Third World. The buyers come here and tell us that we should not let children work in the mines. I say to them, "Sure, that is OK in the West. But what would you have the children do here in Congo?" There is no school for them here like there is in the West. Just look outside. You will see children working everywhere. If they do not work, then how are they going to earn money for food? Who is going to feed them? Not you.'

I'm intrigued enough by Panju's tales of cross-border smuggling to make my way down to the Ruzizi river, which flows down from the Itombe mountains into Lake Kivu and forms the border between the Democratic Republic of Congo and Rwanda. All along its western shore are shanty houses of mud brick and corrugated-iron roofs that face across the short distance to where life is unfathomably different. Here on the shore next to town the span is around 60 metres, but there are bends and turns all along the river as far as Lake Tanganyika, where you could throw a stone from Congo and it would land in Rwanda.

Satari has a small stall selling bottles of Safari, the local beer brewed here in Bukavu. My hotel is directly opposite his stall and, because a family of devout Protestants run it, there is a self-imposed ban on the sale of alcohol. So Satari and I have established a routine whereby every evening I buy a couple of bottles of Safari from his stall and return the empties from the previous night. The first evening, I didn't have any empties and Satari took some persuading that I would indeed return with them the next day. I think the experience brought us closer together.

Satari's house is down the hill close to the water. From his house he gets a good view of the late-night activities on the river. 'Every night,' he tells me, 'people are smuggling things both ways. They even bring goats from Rwanda to Congo because they are cheaper over there. Sometimes if they have no boat they will even swim across with them. It is dangerous and often people drown. We see bodies washed up on the shore often. Very often.'

But the biggest trade across the river is minerals. 'When we are sleeping sometimes I can wake when I hear them cry out across the river. Then I will hear a cry from the other side – that is how they know it is time to cross.' He nods to impress on me that this is serious. This is not goat smuggling. 'Sometimes you can even see them. When I was coming back from my cousin's wedding last month, my brother and I could hear the truck coming up the road beside the river. It stopped and many fishermen who have boats by the river came and started to unload it. They were carrying big sacks of minerals down to the river and then when the boats were ready, with four or five heavy sacks in each boat, I would say at least ten tonnes in total, they paddled them to the other side. But this is very dangerous.' His nod has turned to a cautionary shake. 'If you do not know the river well then you can drown. A boy I know, my friend, died this way last month too. He was sixteen years old – his name was Joussaint Kayabu. He was smuggling minerals to Rwanda.'

Drowning is common on the river, but sometimes the bodies wash up with bullet holes in them. The Congolese army carefully controls the crossing and the smugglers must pay the right person on the stretch of river that they are using. Often disputes over territory result in people being made an example of, and a washed-up corpse is the perfect way to deliver the message.

This is not a recent development in the Congolese mineral trade, but Satari says it is becoming increasingly common. The recent pressure put on suppliers to stop exporting 'unethical' minerals has only forced the trade underground so that instead the same minerals are being smuggled into Rwanda from where they can be 'ethically' exported. The UN encourages the international community to put the trade in Congolese minerals 'on hold' while it continues its struggle to find a peaceful resolution to the conflict here, but the people have to continue selling their minerals to make their living. And if they can't sell them openly, their only choice is to come down to the Ruzizi river after dark. Unwittingly perhaps we have added another deadly link into an already ruthless supply chain.

As for the Chinese trade route, and the ever-growing might of China, this becomes increasingly apparent the further I start to move away from Bukavu. At first the road isn't much of a road; it is more of a long cabbage patch, albeit without any cabbages. The storms of the previous night are beginning to recede, but a fine veil of rain hangs over the area and it gets mistier and muddier as we climb the hills that lead south-west out of the town. Along the roadside there is a steady stream of folk, all carrying items on their heads. Men and women carry piles of bananas, heavy buckets of water and even long thick pieces of firewood, balanced precariously while they try not to slide head over heels into the wet mud. By the side of the road small, roughly assembled tables display bananas, potatoes and yams for sale and next to them tiny piles of charcoal; enough to keep a fire going for just long enough to cook them.

As we get further away from Bukavu, however, the road gets steadily better. It turns out that we are following the route made by a team of Chinese road builders who came here two years ago to build a road from Bukavu through Kamituga 180 kilometres away and then beyond to Kindu. The further from Bukavu we go, the more recently the Chinese road builders have been here and so the better the road. At this rate I am fully anticipating a six-lane highway by the time we reach Kamituga, but in fact it is more an indication that no one has taken responsibility for maintaining the road since it was built.

The Chinese road is part of a $5 billion deal for infrastructure between China and the Democratic Republic of Congo. Many Western companies were burned during Congo's wars, and given the scale of the recession that has hit Western companies and their potential for new investment they have been a little slow to come back. Not so China. China generates an annual trade surplus of some $200 billion, and what is it going to do with it? As I saw in Laos, rather than sit on it and watch it slowly devalue with the crumbling dollar, China is actively investing in its own future – not just in neighbouring countries like Laos, but also here; for example, in DRC a loan to rebuild the roads will be paid back by way of lucrative and exclusive mining contracts.

China is eyeing up the prize of the world's richest assortment of minerals. On the face of it, the $5 billion received by DRC seems to be helping to rebuild Congo's decayed infrastructure: as well as here on the new road to Kamituga, there are new roads and rail lines being constructed to link the mineral-rich areas of eastern and southern Congo. This new road will link up with a 3,400-kilometre highway between the north-east city of Kisangani and Kasumbalesa on Congo's southern border with Zambia.

These roads of course facilitate the extraction of Congo's minerals, but when you look at the direction in which they are taking them you can start to see how they betray the Chinese game plan and a new Chinese perspective on the world. Congo's new Chinese-built road and rail map gives a clear indication of how China is redrawing the economic map in central and southern Africa, linking their new mining interests in Congo to more established Chinese-built networks in Zambia and Angola as well as the Atlantic port at Matadi DRC, thereby redirecting the country's huge mineral potential away from South Africa, seen as too deeply involved with the West. This is not development with

Congo's interests at heart but rather a calculated scheme to further China's economic self-interest.

Either side of the new road it is still not safe. The FDLR continue to be operational in areas of South Kivu and you take your life in your own hands should you stray more than a kilometre from the road. The result is that villages are built all along our route close to the safety of the road and the security that its traffic brings. Most of that traffic consists of NGO four-wheel-drive vehicles, Pakistani UN peacekeepers in white Land Rovers and large trucks loaded first with hessian sacks and then loaded again with people on top of the sacks.

Like other African countries I have travelled in, the road is frequently barred by checkpoints where Congolese soldiers find faults with either the vehicle or the paperwork of the passengers inside. For the middlemen bringing minerals into the sale houses from town it is where they pay 'taxes' – in fact more like extorted payments demanded by these men with guns who control the roads; extracting a few dollars boosts their wages. I am well used to it and fully expect it. In fact I have even prepared a bundle of small notes with which to grease the necessary palms along the way, but we seem to be sailing through checkpoint after checkpoint without any hassle whatsoever.

'They think you're a priest,' laughs Amani. The car we have hired belongs to a Congolese guy in town but he bought it from a French NGO, AFEM, who worked frequently with priests. It seems that people still recognise the car and have assumed that the white guy in the black top (my fleece) must be a priest. I can't help but laugh too. I've been mistaken for many things but this is the first time anyone has taken me to be a minister of the cloth. 'It's funny but it's good,' smiles Amani from the back seat. 'If there was no priest in the car then they would ask for money every time.' This is great. I even relax into my role enough to offer a few blessings out of the window.

Nowhere is there such a presence of NGOs as in the Democratic Republic of Congo. I wonder if they are all here out of a collective sense of Western guilt after the colonial era helped make such a mess of the place. Every couple of miles there is a village and in every village there is at least one large faded white sign. The signs bear the logos of various NGOs and below each logo there is an explanation of the project that the NGO have sponsored in the village. Many of the signs seem quite old.

At the next village, I stop and get out to take a closer look at its sign. It has been erected by a relatively small Belgian NGO and heralds the construction of a village school. Around the corner there is indeed a single-storey building, remarkable in that it is the only building in the village built from bricks and with a corrugated roof. All the other houses here are made from mud and thatch. A couple of curious children watch me closely as I take a picture. It strikes me that they are not in the school, and from the state of them it looks as though they have been playing all day in the mud. I decide to ask them, 'What is this building?'

'It is the school,' the older child answers. I guess she is around eight years old.

'Why are you not there?' I ask, suddenly feeling like a truancy officer.

'There is no teacher.' She's off the hook.

'When was the last time you went to school?'

'I have never been to school. The teacher left before I was old enough to go.'

She says this to me as she stands below the sign. Why is the sign still here? Who is the sign for? I feel annoyed that anyone passing this sign would be left with the wrong impression, that this village already had a school. It hasn't. It still needs a school. What it doesn't need is a new sign.

The next village has a similar story. As I stand facing a sign that tells how USAID and the Catholic Relief Services have built a pump to bring water to the community, I watch a small boy, no older than four, labouring up the hill with a heavy two-gallon container full of water on his back, the strap wrapped around his forehead. I ask a man sitting outside his house, 'Why is the boy carrying water if you have a water pump?'

'The pump has not worked for a long time,' the man tells me. He seems confused.

'Is it not possible for someone to fix it?' I ask, trying to sound somehow constructive.

'No one has come to fix it,' he explains. It seems so tragic, but there is the reality. No one in the community has the know-how to fix the pump. Nobody has come to fix it.

The water pump project was most probably funded to build the pump but simply that. No training of anyone to maintain it and no maintenance offered either. Yet here still is the sign. 'Why don't you take down this sign?' I ask him again. It seems, if nothing else, to be rather inconveniently placed right outside his front door. 'Now that the pump doesn't work,' I offer him as a justification for my question.

'It is not my sign,' he says, shrugging as if to say it was a ridiculous suggestion in the first place.

I get back into the car. All the way to Mwenga, we pass along the red mud road up and through the villages of the Mitumba mountains. Every turn reveals a patchwork of fields in the valley below, surrounded on all sides by thick jungle, and every village has its NGO signs trying to boast of success but really just highlighting the failure of NGOs in DRC to really effect any palpable and sustainable change on the ground. Congo is clearly still a dirt poor place to live and I just want to tear down all of these self-congratulatory signs trying to somehow convince me otherwise.

A few of the children along the road have been making a funny noise when they have seen me. At first I think it sounds like the heehaw noise of a donkey, for which I can come up with no explanation, but then one of the children starts saying, '*Chinois, Chinois.*' Suddenly I realise that what they have been saying isn't 'heehaw' but '*Ni hao*'. They are saying hello to me in Chinese. They think that I am Chinese! First a priest, and now this!

Up until the last ten years, a few Western companies held ultimate power over the market for Africa's natural resources. They were the only show in town, whether for oil, food or minerals, and could call the shots on how much was wanted and what prices were going to be paid. The changing landscape of ethical consumerism in the West may have put pressure on its companies to embargo minerals sourced from countries like DRC but that doesn't stop the trade. There will always be buyers in town who aren't concerned about our ethical agenda.

Now the Chinese are calling the shots, and, as in Laos, the interests of the producers are not exactly the first thing on their minds. But that doesn't let the West off the hook. The supply of DRC's most valuable resources, cassiterite and coltan, is driven by increasing demand from the Western electronics industry. Once exported from Congo the main smelting and processing companies that transform the minerals into usable components are Thaisarco, owned by British company AMC, British-owned Afrimex, Belgian Trademet and Traxys and Panju's main customer, Malaysian MSC, all of whom have been cited by the UN as having bought minerals 'from *comptoirs* who in turn work closely with armed groups'.

These trading and processing companies use many explanations to mitigate their involvement in the dark side of the mineral trade. They range from the innocent ('[We only acquire] through licensed traders who are authorised to perform the trade [and have] confirmed that the material arises from legitimate sources' (MSC)) to the 'ethical' ('Continued trade in minerals from DRC is fundamental to the well-being of artisanal mining communities' (Thaisarco)), to the despairing ('To verify the exact origin of every kilo of exported material . . . was the exclusive responsibility of the Congolese state not that of companies like Trademet' (Trademet)).

And from these companies we move to some household names – Apple, Nokia, Motorola and Dell, to name a few. All are aware of the problem. An official statement from Nokia, for example, acknowledged that this is an issue for which it must accept some responsibility and even effect some change.

> Nokia is concerned about poor practices at some mine operations around the world, not just in the DRC. Nokia is in a position to positively influence our supply chain, promoting high environmental and social standards . . . If we find that standards are not being met we do not walk away but work with that supplier to address the issues and in so doing help to raise overall standards. (Nokia 2009)

In the same year the electronics industry as a whole asked its trade association, the International Tin Research Institute (ITRI), to coordinate 'a comprehensive due diligence plan for tin minerals exported from DRC to address concerns over "conflict minerals" from the region'. The plan has the support of most of the main consumers in the electronics sector, such as Apple, Dell, HP, IBM, Intel, Microsoft, Motorola, Nokia, Philips, Sony, Telefónica, Western Digital and Xerox.

Unfortunately the ITRI plan does not deal specifically with the trade of minerals with armed groups, nor does it even begin to address the conditions in which the miners are operating. It is a document of soft and toothless platitudes that talk of 'recognising' issues, 'encouraging' change and expressing 'concern' for circumstances, but nowhere does it set out accountable and transparent agendas for effecting measurable change. A coordinated giant corporate action would of course be welcome, but not if it's a smokescreen aimed only at throwing concerned consumers and vigilant campaigners off the scent. Ultimately each company has enormous power to enforce rules that could put pressure on the unscrupulous middlemen who act to muddy the waters of the supply chain and prolong the conflict for their own nefarious ends. The current set-up gives little cause for celebration.

I was starting to realise that we have a real fight on our hands. Western companies in Asia and here in the dark heart of Africa are operating on the front line, and the lives of some of the poorest people in the world are at stake. But these are not the only places where Western ethical values are being played out and lives are being put at risk.

6

Poppycock

Afghanistan: Rubat Sangi

'If you want to be a real trader and you want to love your country you have to be smart'

At 6 a.m. we eventually catch sight of the heavily armed vehicles that make up the convoy of Afghan National Police (ANP) and Counter Narcotics. The line is heading north out of Herat. We are around 50 kilometres from the Turkmenistan border. My driver Mahmood has a beat-up old Toyota, which got a flat on the way out of town so we had to fall behind while he changed the tyre. The Minister of Counter Narcotics, Mr Daqiq, had warned me that the road to Rubat Sangi was not safe to travel alone and that we must go with the armed convoy. So I feel relieved when Mahmood's Toyota catches up and pulls in behind a green ANP pickup truck. The truck is loaded with young policemen toting Kalashnikov AK-47 assault rifles and rocket launchers. The dusty desert road ahead has forced many of them to pull their scarves up over their faces so that they take on a menacing look and I have to remind myself that these are the good guys.

At the district centre we rendezvous with a unit from the US 82nd Airborne Division and our convoy takes on another eight vehicles: desert-camouflaged armoured Humvees decorated with heavy machine guns. Ash, a lance corporal in the front of one of the armoured vehicles, has been in the country for eight months now. 'Things have been pretty quiet recently,' he explains in a slow

Carolina drawl. 'I guess the Taliban have been busy in the fields with the harvest or whatever. But we're expecting things to get a little hotter real soon.'

The vehicles begin the drive further north and we are now a full army battalion plus one red 1992 Toyota Corolla. We move carefully along the road, climbing further up into a barren, rocky mountainous landscape and towards the remote village areas closer to the border. The only other traffic we pass consists of oil tankers bringing fuel in the opposite direction, each one flanked fore and aft by heavily armed private security vehicles.

We turn off the road into a dusty desert track. The US Humvees in front kick up clouds of dust so that Mahmood can only guess at what's ahead. Last week Taliban insurgents fired upon a similar poppy eradication mission in Nangahar, killing three police officers and wounding four others. It is no secret that the Taliban have vested financial interests in poppy cultivation in Afghanistan and fund many of their activities from the profits. The poppy police are as much the enemy as the US soldiers sent to protect them.

My translator Asif is turning around in the front seat and chatting happily with me about my impressions of his country. I notice that on his left hand the line of his index finger continues straight down to his wrist, so where his thumb should be there is only a scar. He also has a very prominent circular scar on his cheek and another similar scar just below the ear.

'Last year I was driving on the road to Kabul to go to my cousin's wedding,' he tells me. 'I was stopped by Taliban. At first I thought they were bandits and I was going to be robbed but then they opened fire on me. I was shot eleven times.' He begins to show me the scars. It seems that hiding below each sleeve and trouser leg is another bullet hole.

'I am lucky to be alive,' he says, 'but I now want only to live somewhere else. Somewhere that is not Afghanistan.' The Taliban have destroyed much in Afghanistan, but nothing more significant than the hope of a generation. The country desperately needs bright young men like Asif to remain here, to invest in its future, to rebuild the country and its economy.

We bump along in the Toyota over the dirt road behind the Hummers until we reach the top of a hill that looks across a vast flat valley. In the bright blue sky above, a few fluffy clouds meander their way over the scorched dry hills to the north. The valley is a patchwork of green irrigated wheat fields and for a moment I feel that I could be in the English countryside at the end of a particularly hot summer. But as my eyes adjust I begin to notice four or five small villages built into the distant hills. They were not initially visible, as the mud from which they are built is the same colour as the earth, but slowly they emerge from the background until I can see them all clearly and I wonder how I ever couldn't.

The senior officers of the US Airborne, ANP, Counter Narcotics and the Afghan army have gathered together with an auxiliary team of translators to discuss strategy. It is proposed that, as the mission is being led by Counter Narcotics, it should be the minister himself fronting up the team, with support from the ANP. This lead unit will go village to village eradicating fields that have been planted with poppy. The US Airborne and Afghan army units will take up strategic positions in the surrounding area high above the villages and will be on hand in the event of anti-eradication resistance. I will travel with the minister.

We re-establish the convoy and make our way along the dirt track leading into the village of Kakatoot. The centre of the village has a small clearing where three small white tents have been erected. This is the school. A group of older bearded men press their backs close to a wall, using the narrow shadow to shield them from the sun. Afghan houses are traditionally surrounded by a head-high mud wall so that villages like this one take on a labyrinthine quality. Behind each wall, as well as the house, is some land on which to grow crops.

The ANP captain begins to make his way from house to house, peeking over the walls or through the cracks in the doors. He is looking for the familiar telltale sign of bright pink flowers growing behind. When he lets out a cry and holds his hand aloft, two of his men come running and on his command they begin to kick down the door. When it eventually comes away from its hinges, he gives a hurried glance inside and then he barks an order for the patrol to move into the house. His men proceed, scanning up and down the walls with the barrels of their guns. This is the time when they (and I) are most likely to come under attack.

As we move into the field, armed police begin to take up positions on the roofs of neighbouring houses, training their guns on potential points from which we could be attacked. Finally the captain shouts out that the field is secure and the remaining officers march in. The Taliban often booby-trap poppy fields if they suspect eradication is imminent, so two soldiers are sent in to look for signs of mines or improvised explosive devices (IEDs). Eventually they determine that the field is clean and eradication can begin. This is by no means a high-tech operation. The policemen each hold an AK-47 in one hand and a long stick in the other. They begin to swish their way through the fields, removing the heads from the pretty pink flowers. Even the minister is enthusiastically having a go.

Within a few minutes, the single-jerib (0.2-hectare) field of opium has been cleared, and the world contains around a kilo less heroin.

The poppy eradication programme has been going on for years now; since 2002 Western governments have spent over $5 billion on it. That's a vast sum of money, which I, like most people, have always assumed was money well spent. Afghanistan, after all, is responsible for producing over 90 per cent of the world's heroin, and heroin is self-evidently a curse. Its destructive effects are felt the world over. From Russia to Iran to Europe to the United States, shivering and desperate drug addicts can be found on the streets of every modern city, turning to crime to feed their habit and condemning themselves to often brutally short lives. Anything that can be done to cut the supply has to be welcomed.

And, of course, there are also the people behind the trade: the drug barons, cartels and criminal middlemen who grow rich on human misery. In the case of Afghanistan, many of those people come from the ranks of the Taliban. The UK government have often claimed that as much as 25 per cent of the Taliban's total funding comes from opium. At first glance, if ever there was a case for a drugs eradication programme, Afghanistan would seem to be the prime candidate.

However, as I have found elsewhere on my travels, things are not always simple. When you have first-hand experiences in these places and dig a little deeper it seems that eradication is at best too pat a solution; at worst, it's actually counterproductive.

Let's start by looking at that figure of 25 per cent funding for the Taliban. It is derived from a United Nations Office on Drugs and

Crime (UNODC) report, which estimates that anti-government elements (AGEs) collectively profit by over $300 million from the trade in illegal opium every year.

The UNODC report is careful to clarify that this is not money being earned exclusively by the Taliban. In fact, it is misleading to class all AGEs as Taliban when most of the opium profits are actually being made by warlords and drug lords with no connection to the Taliban. The UNODC also point out that as most of the Taliban revenues from opium are in fact derived from *ushr*, a tax, which they impose on all agricultural products in the areas they control, they would make just as much money from wheat or any other crop.

Paradoxically, there is even evidence that eradication actually helps the warlords. The World Bank, for instance, have complained that it helps drive up the 'risk premium', which in turn pushes farm-gate prices higher and causes 'greater extortion of "protection money" from farmers by various authorities'. And while eradication has had profound repercussions for the individual farmers targeted, its overall effect on national production has been marginal and has 'accounted for only a very small proportion of the decrease in cultivated area'. It also creates an opportunity for corruption: 'There are serious concerns that, due to the close ties between many local officials and drug interests, Governor-led eradication is especially vulnerable to corruption in implementation.'

A further paradox is that in the south of the country, where the most aggressive eradication has taken place, such Taliban strongholds as Helmand and Kandahar are producing more poppies than ever. Only a naturally occurring poppy blight has made any real dent on production in the past ten years. The relatively fluid border with Pakistan allows easy smuggling routes for the traffickers, and Helmand, Farah and Kandahar produced over 3,000 of the total estimated national yield of 3,600 tonnes for 2010.

For now poppy production in Herat continues in two troublesome districts: Shindand in the south-west and Rubat Sangi to the north. In both areas Taliban and Turkmen mafia groups remain active. The Minister for Counter Narcotics, Mr Daqiq, explains: 'Already we have had nine policemen killed and another twenty injured in our eradication programme this year. The mafia groups that profit from the trade in the drug are encouraging farmers to grow poppy and they can often try to fight against the eradication.' Then, almost as an afterthought, he adds, 'But we are always a step ahead of the mafia.'

The farmers often take a down payment on their opium harvest in advance from the illegal groups. They are dependent on the advance to see them through the harsh winter months when nothing will grow in their fields. The drug smugglers will visit them on their farms and offer them support in exchange for their commitment to supply them opium in the spring. 'They can take twenty dollars per kilogram in advance from a trafficker and then they are bound in to the contract,' says Mr Daqiq.

But the plight of the farmer does not seem to concern him too much. He has his own financial headache to contend with. 'The eradication is paid for by the Americans and the British but they only pay us 135 dollars for every hectare eradicated. We cannot travel 200 kilometres away if we are only going to eradicate four hectares. This does not make economic sense. Sure, last year we eradicated several hundred hectares but this year we don't expect so much. But we have to do it anyway otherwise the people will think it is OK to go back to poppy.'

*

To see for myself what all this means for the individual farmer, I seek out one of those whose crops have been destroyed by the eradication team today – a local man, Hagi Jan. Hagi is talking with the Counter Narcotics forces back in the village. He is tall and charismatic with a black turban and a long distinguished grey beard. The deep, dark lines of his face frame a pair of piercing emerald-green eyes that at first sight detract attention from his left shirtsleeve draping loosely off his shoulder. Hagi lost his arm fighting the Russians with the mujahideen in the 1990s. Now he is a farmer and village elder.

From where we stand – a hill in the centre of the village – I can see the extent to which the scheme to encourage farmers into alternative crops has been successful. Many of the fields below are planted with wheat that is now almost ready for harvest next month. The policemen who came here last year tell me that then it was different; then they were mostly poppy. Rising international wheat prices have encouraged farmers to switch (some have even torn out old vegetable crop fields too in pursuit of a bigger slice of the rise of wheat). But Afghanistan is a country that experiences climatic extremes and long memories. Farmers here remember too that two years ago the spring rains failed, and those who had grown wheat, which is dependent on high rainfall, fared badly. Little wonder then that still many have held off and are persisting with the 'safer' option of an illicit opium crop.

'We have lost six jeribs (1.2 hectares) of poppy today,' Hagi Jan tells me with a rueful smile. 'If they had not destroyed this, our village would have had over forty kilograms of opium to sell when the buyers came here.' He shakes his head. 'That is over 3,000 US dollars. Now some of the young men from the village will have to go to Iran to find work. Otherwise how will they feed their families?'

Like farmers in any country, what an Afghan farmer chooses to put in the ground is never simply a case of picking the crop with the highest current price. Farmers also have to balance growing enough food to eat with the need to allocate some land to cash crops to bring in the necessary income to buy other staples that they can't grow, or to supplement what they can. This is particularly true when food prices are rising, as they are all over the world.

The decisions faced by farmers in other parts of the world are even more complicated in Afghanistan. Even if farmers here can grow enough produce to have some left over to sell, they have to get it to market and that means travelling through areas that are not secure. These farmers don't have the benefit of an American 82nd Airborne Division escort on market day. 'If we take crops to sell at the market we can be stopped by the Taliban, the Afghanistan National Police or thieves. Then we end up with nothing. Better to grow poppy. Then the traders come to you.' Hagi has done his risk assessment and it leads to one conclusion – opium poppy.

Hagi and the other farmers here must also consider that the drug traffickers pay cash and collect. The security situation here can be so bad that a farmer growing a crop like wheat has to take it through several checkpoints to get it to market. 'Each one of these checkpoints can ask you for a bribe. So then when you get to the market, all your profit is already gone. But with poppy we don't have to leave our village. Many farmers in the village would grow other crops if we had better security. Even if it meant we made less money we would do that but there is a limit. We cannot do that if it means we do not have enough to eat.'

There is a clear link between security and opium production in Afghanistan. The regions of the country that have improved safety have simultaneously created an environment more conducive to trade. In the northern districts, where farmers are safe to travel to market, there is an incentive to grow crops other than opium for the drug lords. Arguably, pumping international money into securing highways would have a more beneficial effect than channelling it into direct counter-narcotic strategies like eradication.

When the Counter Narcotics team are safely out of earshot, I ask Hagi why he thinks they are destroying his crops today. Hagi explains to me that the people like him in the village are poor and they have no choice but to grow poppies; without help from the government to buy seeds for other crops, there is no alternative. He suggests that we go back to his house to continue the conversation there. I assume he means because it will be more private, so I am a little surprised when we get to Hagi's house and I find all the senior members of the eradication team already tucking into a lunch that he has provided.

'Even if my enemy who had killed my son came to my house,' he explains, 'I would still offer him tea and bread. This is our culture. Most of the policemen who have come here are even my own friends.' The men sitting around the table nod their approval, while Hagi continues to make his case. 'In our culture growing opium is *haram* (forbidden in the Koran) and many people do not agree that we should even be growing it. But we have no money for seeds for other crops and the government do not give us these seeds so what are we to do? If we have a field with nothing to grow in it then we must grow poppies. If they come again next year then they will find some people will grow poppy again. Better for them to take their chances than to just leave a field empty.'

Incredibly, in the period from 1994 to 1999 Afghanistan managed to double its opium crop. In a way, its farmers deserve credit for this: they had to borrow cash up front, repay loans with interest and reinvest for next year's harvest at a time of continual and devastating war. We may disapprove of what they were growing, but the fact remains that they were able to keep their families alive through the winter, and gradually cultivate additional land. It is easy to miss the sheer determination, imagination and shrewd entrepreneurialism of these uneducated men.

When our lunch is finished, the minister asks that he and Hagi be left alone. They have some business to discuss. I am not welcome to stay. I wait outside for half an hour and when Hagi emerges with the minister there are smiles all round. It would seem that the minister has given Hagi some good news. What that might be he is not willing to say.

So, is there another solution?

Some analysts point to the experience of Turkey back in the 1970s as a possible way forward for Afghanistan. Back then, Turkey was notorious as the principal source of the global heroin trade: in fact, by 1970, over 80 per cent of the heroin smuggled into the United States was grown as opium poppies on Turkey's western Anatolian plains. From there it was smuggled as far as Marseilles for processing into heroin before being shipped across the Atlantic. Marseilles was a key hub for the Corsican mafia gangs who controlled the trade of hundreds of millions of dollars' worth of heroin from Turkey – the so-called French Connection.

What changed things was the pressure placed on the Turkish government by the country with whom Turkey had perhaps its strongest military and economic ties: the United States. In June

1971, following negotiations with President Nixon, the Turkish prime minister announced a total ban on poppy cultivation, which was enforced the subsequent year. The US offered $35 million in compensation. The plan was a success for Turkey, albeit that the international trade in heroin barely broke stride as other countries, first Mexico and then South East Asia, quickly stepped in to supply demand. Nevertheless Turkey was rewarded for its efforts.

Having established control of their country's production, and with the drug lords moved on elsewhere to look for their supply of raw opium, Turkey's government was able to revisit the idea of growing the crop but this time for legitimate purposes.

Then in 1981 the US government passed legislation to give 'special protected market status' to Turkey and India under what became known as the 80/20 Rule. This guaranteed the two opium-producing states that the world's largest consumer of opiate-based medicines, the United States, would commit to purchasing 80 per cent of all its raw opium imports from them. This arrangement has remained in place ever since and continues today. The result is that the Turkish coffers are enriched to the tune of around $60 million annually. Thus Turkey has made the transition from being the world's largest illicit supplier of opium to one of the world's top four legitimate producers of poppies for opiate-based medicines, based on a carefully controlled, licensed poppy cultivation programme.

In 2005, the Senlis Council, a research 'think tank' (of which there are scores in Afghanistan), proposed a new solution to the issue of Afghanistan's economic development and its central role in the supply of the world's heroin. Why, Senlis asked, don't the international community simply buy up all the Afghan opium poppies for the production of opiate-based painkillers such as morphine, rather as happened with Turkey back in the 1980s?

These painkillers could then be sold in the developing world, in particular in Latin America.

Sadly, of course, life is never quite as simple as that. The fact that there's a global need for more morphine doesn't mean that the demand is necessarily there. Currently 80 per cent of the world's opiate-based painkillers are consumed by only six of the world's richest countries: the United States, the UK, Canada, Australia, France and Germany. For now, vast swathes of Africa, Asia and Latin America (80 per cent of the global population) remain almost free (6 per cent of global supply) of opiate-based pain relief. They might want pain relief, but paying for it is a problem.

Nevertheless, there may be something in the idea of legitimising some of the Afghan supply. At present, over 90 per cent of the global supply of legitimate opium comes from only four countries: India, Australia, Turkey and France. The poppies from these countries are turned into painkillers like morphine and codeine by a small number of Western pharmaceuticals, such as British giants GlaxoSmithKline and Johnson Matthey and the US corporate Johnson & Johnson. Some countries adopt a high-tech approach to opium production, but Indian farmers, for example, produce it in much the same old-fashioned way as farmers in Afghanistan, and make a good living out of it. Essentially, they extract the opium latex by hand from the bulbous heads of the poppy plants and then leave it to dry in the sun until it becomes brown and sticky.

Indian farmers are rewarded for producing higher yields with higher prices per kilogram. So if a farmer grows, say, 40 kilos of opium and sells it all to the government like he's supposed to, then he receives $50 per kilo. However, if he was tempted to keep, say, 10 kilos to one side to sell to an illicit drug trafficker, he would receive only $30 per kilo from the government for the remainder.

The farmers are thereby incentivised to sell all of their produce to the government rather than squirrelling some off to sell on the illicit market.

It is tempting to ask, therefore, why Afghanistan is not allowed to compete with the countries already supplying morphine, in particular the country that supplies the wet opium form that most Afghan farmers understand, India. In 2005 India was granted a licence by the International Narcotics Control Board (INCB) to produce up to 1,200 tonnes of opium annually. This meant that the Indian government could grant opium-growing licences to some 16,000 farmers to cultivate opium on around 35,000 hectares of their land. In 2007 the INCB reported exports of raw opium from India at just over 600 tonnes. The United States imported 500 of these and Japan took the bulk of the remaining 100. That's 600 tonnes that could easily have been supplied by Afghanistan.

The reason that the United States remains the biggest purchaser of Indian opium is the 80/20 Rule which requires all US opiate-based pharmaceutical companies such as Mallinckrodt and Noramco to buy at least 80 per cent of their opiate from India and Turkey. One is left wondering whether the money spent on ineffectual poppy eradication in Afghanistan might not be better channelled into encouraging Indian farmers to diversify their crops while Afghanistan is given a chance to improve its lot.

Another way forward presents itself when I visit Herat, Afghanistan's westernmost province, which borders Iran to the west and Turkmenistan to the north. The city is arranged around its castle, originally built by Alexander the Great and now lovingly restored by the Aga Khan Foundation, and is towered over by its famous minarets which reach high up through the pollution into the dusty sky. There were once 12 minarets, but various wars have reduced the total to only five. The fifth leans over so precariously that it seems that the traffic thundering past could cause it to topple.

In Herat, the people are Tajik, unlike the mostly Pashtun population of Kabul. The border is only 90 miles away. The people of Herat have always had an air of superiority over their countrymen in the capital. The toothless old men who sit on stools outside their shops proudly boast that while Kabul has become a dysfunctional enclave for expats and corrupt politicians, Herat enjoys 24-hour electricity, paved roads and a thriving commercial district. Last year Herat contributed over $240 million in tax revenues to the capital, by far the biggest contribution by any region. Herat, they will tell you, has always been a town of traders.

Ghafar Hamidzai sits behind an enormous desk in his office overlooking the centre of town. He is only 24 years old, but already one of the country's most successful businessmen. Ghafar's company, Afghan Saffron, is the country's largest exporter of saffron, a crop that was almost unknown in Afghanistan as recently as five years ago. Ghafar has had big plans right from the business's slightly unorthodox beginning.

'We smuggled 500 tonnes of corms (saffron bulbs) from Iran four years ago,' Ghafar says. 'We tried to deal with the Iranians officially but they didn't want to share their business with Afghanistan.' His face cracks into a smile. 'If you want to be a real trader and you want to love your country you have to be so smart,' he laughs.

To start growing saffron a farmer has to plant around 2.5 tonnes of corms for each hectare. For most farmers in the region, land is divided up into jeribs (around 0.2 hectares), and the norm is for a smallholder to cultivate two jeribs. This means that for a farmer to make a decent go of farming saffron he needs half a tonne (500 kilograms) of corms to get him going. This year the international community through NATO's Provincial Reconstruction Teams is offering a total of only 50 tonnes of corms for free to farmers, enough for 100 jeribs. With over 1,000 farmers registering interest in switching from poppy to saffron, it's safe to say there will be a lot of disappointed farmers. Ghafar, on the other hand, has already distributed ten times as much with his smuggled corms, which he sells for $2 per kilo.

'We offer what we call a "Complete Saffron Package" which includes the corm as well as advice on how to plant, cultivate and harvest and how to market and sell once the saffron is ready.' He speaks like a true salesman. 'We now have the facility in two laboratories that we have built here in Herat to have the saffron tested and certified. For the best saffron we can offer our farmers 1,500 to even 2,500 dollars per kilogram for the very best saffron in the world.'

And he's not kidding. Currently the global production of saffron is around 300 tonnes annually of which roughly 90 per cent comes from Iran. The Iranian harvest has had a torrid couple of years recently which has seen the international wholesale price of saffron rocket to over $3,000 per kilo. The very best stuff can reach double that. Iran alone pulls in over $300 million in revenues from saffron.

Afghanistan's contribution to this global supply is still pretty small. Around 500 kilograms were exported in 2009, but Ghafar believes that could easily double in 2010. It's the lack of supply holding him back and that means getting farmers enough access to corms. Ghafar is confident that there is a market for considerably more Afghan saffron than the country is currently producing.

One farmer to benefit from Ghafar's enterprise is Hagi Ibrahim, a Pashtun farmer with a long grey beard and a black and white striped turban that sits a little askew on his head. He has come into Herat to visit the Ministry of Agriculture for a lesson on how to select the best saffron from the rest so he can sell it for the highest price. In his village, Gulmir, to the east of Herat, Ibrahim heads up a cooperative that has 5 hectares under cultivation, half wheat and half saffron. Four years ago it was 100 per cent opium. 'You need security when you grow opium. Always there is danger,' he says. 'But even so, we were reluctant to switch to saffron because it is new but when we saw other farmers were making good money, we wanted to do it also.' The Ministry of Agriculture provides training for the farmers at their centre, but Ibrahim would like to see them do more. 'The problem is that the government don't give us enough seeds, so some people have even had to sell their cows to buy saffron seeds. But we grow saffron and in our village we have bought a tractor last year.' His heavy gold watch hangs loosely from his wrist; I suspect the tractor isn't the only recent purchase he has made.

Ghafar and Ibrahim are examples of what many international observers as well as Afghans like Asif believe cannot exist in Afghanistan – successful Afghan businessmen. Unfortunately there are not enough and those who are trying are not getting enough support. The poppy farmers in Rubat Sangi would happily plant saffron either alongside or in preference to poppy as Ibrahim has done, if only they had access to the corms or to the credit to buy Ghafar's Complete Saffron Package. As yet, they have neither.

The problem with all top-down solutions, such as eradication, is that they don't take account of the realities or the subtleties of what is really going on. There may actually be a way forward with the opium trade in Afghanistan. Other things being equal, legitimising the Afghan supply would at least create more competition in the legitimate international opium market. If the market were a level playing field, then what would there be to stop an Afghan producer merely competing with an Indian or indeed a European producer?

Might the Afghan farmer still be tempted to sell some of his opium into the illicit market? Well yes, but is that really so much of a problem? Are we really expecting to solve the world's heroin addiction by trashing a few farmers' fields here in Herat? As long as there is demand for heroin on the streets of New York and London then someone will supply it. What we should really be concerned about is how we help the Afghan farmer to make a living so that he doesn't have to take loans from the Taliban or other warlords, or risk blowing himself up on a mine laid in his fields.

There is a real opportunity here for the international community to think the way Bill Valentino, the CSR specialist I'd met in China, describes as 'right-brained'. Afghanistan needs the kind of sustainable projects that can tie the country in to Western capitalism. I am sure there is a long line of Chinese investors waiting to fill the gap if not. In fact, a new copper mine south of Kabul that was opened recently with Chinese money suggests they already have.

The goal should be to draw the farmers out of the black and into the real economy – this is what state building depends on. Any strategy needs to encourage farmers to move some of their cultivation into legitimate crops. Of course there is a need in Afghanistan for more staples to be home-grown; the wheat fields of Rubat Sangi are testament to the fact that this need is being acknowledged. But farmers also need cash crops, and if that is no longer to be opium then it needs to be something else.

Decades of war have denied farmers credit from any sources other than opium traffickers and therefore pushed them into opium cultivation for illicit use. The cycle needs to be broken by giving farmers like Hagi access to credit and alternative cash crops such as saffron, as well as access to markets for their produce, such as the big saffron-consuming countries in the West – the United States and Spain. As Ibrahim the saffron farmer from Herat pointed out, farmers making a legitimate income do not require security and so do not rely so heavily on the gun.

Sadly, though, because this approach falls outside the Grand Plan, it isn't receiving enough support. The problem is that our priority in Afghanistan is all wrong. It is Afghanistan's continuing poverty that creates the necessary environment for drug lords and extremists to operate within. Afghanistan's economy still relies on its agricultural output and it is here that national wealth can be improved. Agricultural output alone could be the spur to promote trade and thereby reduce poverty so as to, in turn, facilitate peace.

But in the meantime, the Afghans continue to suffer, our soldiers' lives continue to be endangered and the war on drugs fails to make any progress. Pursuing what seems like an obvious solution to a very Western social problem like drug abuse, while at the same time fighting the Taliban, looks on paper like a no-brainer. It is in fact a very unethical and unfair policy, which helps no one except maybe those who continue to profit from the opium trade.

7

Do it yourself

Tanzania: Mount Kilimanjaro

'Whenever they're having a problem, I'm having a problem'

I couldn't help wonder whether, between Afghanistan and Gloucestershire (not two places that pop up together very often), I'd seen in Ghafar the saffron entrepreneur and Dave and Ian the ethical coffee merchants something that needed to be looked at more closely. How was it that small businesses were able to behave more ethically, while at the still time making good profits? To look more closely at how the dynamics operated, I decided to follow the supply chain for Dave and Ian's ethical coffee back to its source in Tanzania.

Even for those who live just below it, the snow-capped peak of Mount Kilimanjaro is a rare sight. Africa's highest mountain is so usually shrouded in cloud that I imagine the adventurous few who make it to the very top don't get much of a view. However, if they paused on their way up, at around 6,100 feet, they would get a view of the banana and coffee fields in the centre of Orera village, a collection of approximately 150 households nestled just below the line of the rainforest.

The people who live in Orera are mainly subsistence farmers, and the crops planted along the hillside are mostly the same as they were 50 years ago. Liliani, a young man from the village, tells me how things were very different when he was a child. 'My parents lost confidence in coffee. The prices dropped and they pulled up all the coffee plants to plant more maize and banana. But still my uncles had to leave the village to find work in the town. None of them had trust in coffee. But now we can see the prices rising again and so we got the trust back. Now we are planting coffee again.'

The importance of coffee to the people who live on the mountain cannot be underestimated. This village has suffered greatly over the past 20 years, as a whole generation of men have left the village, never to return. Coffee is the only cash crop here, and Liliani and the other villagers are totally dependent on the price set by the market.

That is until very recently, when the village found a new buyer and began selling its coffee to Ian and Dave and their Ethical Addictions business in Gloucestershire. Remember that Dave and Ian felt they could afford to pay almost twice as much as the farmers had previously received. Up until that point, the village had sold all of its coffee through the local Primary Cooperative – the Kilimanjaro Native Co-operative Union (KNCU) – who then sold it to multinationals like Starbucks.

However, the farmers in Orera like Liliani found that a better deal could be made by turning their backs on the KNCU and instead doing a deal with a small UK company whose packaging doesn't have any ethical logos. But Liliani and the other villagers didn't find a new outlet into the UK coffee market on their own. They benefited from a connection made by one of their neighbours.

Generally, Tanzania has a favourable attitude to foreign direct investment (FDI) and has made significant efforts to encourage it in the past 20 years. The government is also open to expats coming to work in Tanzania, but land ownership remains restrictive. In Tanzania, the state owns all the land. Since the Land Act was passed in 1999, non-citizens cannot buy and own land but instead must lease it from the government through the Tanzania Investment Center (TIC), which has a finite number of designated plots available to foreign investors.

Tanzania is in transition from an economy that was largely public sector run to one in which the private sector will play the leading role. Agriculture is still the major employer – over 80 per cent of the population earn their living from the land.

The farm next to Orera is owned by Bente Luther-Medoc. Bente dresses in hardwearing khaki pants and strong walking boots and her hair is tied up neatly in a ponytail tucked under a khaki soldier's cap. As we walk up the hill towards the boundary of her estate, she looks very much like the old colonialist, a throwback to the days before the war when German farmers ran enormous coffee estates in what was then called Tanganyika. But Bente is a benevolent sort of neo-colonialist.

Having leased around 1,000 acres of land from the socialist government, Bente has transformed a run-down farm into a state-of-the-art coffee estate. She explains that when she moved here she knew 'next to nothing' about coffee, but, having decided to settle here, she set herself the goal of learning all there was to know about coffee cultivation. She drew on expertise from old contacts in Kenya to help get her started and then grafted hard to build up a reputation for growing some of Africa's best coffee.

Bente has to operate within the strict land laws enforced by the Tanzanian government, which means that she pays rent. Every year, on top of the money that Bente invests directly in her farm, she has to pay US$45,000 to the Primary Cooperative. She worries that the people in the surrounding villages don't always understand how much she has had to put in to reach this stage. 'They don't understand reinvestment so they think I'm making shitloads of money,' she laughs, 'and they don't understand the costs of investing to get the farm to this point.' But she hasn't let these misunderstandings fester into resentment.

When she first came to Kilimanjaro, Bente found that the people in the village were also growing coffee but they were not maximising its potential. 'People were still leaving the beans out to dry on any old piece of cloth, sometimes the same one that the baby had peed on.' She screws her face up in disgust at the thought. 'Coffee is very absorbent of smells, so you can imagine what that coffee tasted like.'

The problem for smallholders across the developing world has always been how to improve the quality of their produce to secure higher prices. Improvements require investment, which the farmers either don't know how to find or can't afford themselves. With the best will in the world, if you really want to see improvements in poor rural communities then you have to find a way to inspire change. Or rather someone to inspire change – someone with the know-how and the motivation, who can be there all the time.

During her time living next to Orera and the other neighbouring villages, as well as building up her own farm, Bente has been intent on helping her neighbours. For example, last year she worked with a blacksmith from the local town to design a cooking stove with a chimney. Previously people in the village cooked over an open fire in the centre of their houses, which meant that they lived in a constant fog of smoke. Anyone who has travelled in this part of Africa will recognise the sight of mud huts whose thatched roofs smoulder with black smoke all day long. But Bente's chimneys mean that all the houses in Orera are now smoke-free, and what's more, because the stoves are so much more efficient, the village uses 75 per cent less firewood which has had a massive impact on their deforestation. This is only one of several similarly enlightened initiatives that Bente has taken a lead on.

'The problem with all these projects is that you have to be there at all stages,' she says. 'You can't just give them the money and leave it there.' The village needs to be enabled at all stages. The same goes for their development as quality coffee producers. Bente speaks fluent Swahili, which she thinks is vital to keeping the projects going. 'You have to talk to the people. A lot of projects in Tanzania are getting messed up because the people who run them can't speak Swahili and it's so hard to find a reliable translator – someone who doesn't just give his own opinion or bend the translation.'

In the centre of Orera village, sitting in the shade under the roof of another of those initiatives, a newly constructed coffee sorting shed, a group of around 20 villagers, mainly women and young men, talk with us about how much life in the village has changed recently.

Frida Ngawi, a tall handsome woman wearing a bright orange headscarf and a loose brown shirt, sits picking the shells from cashew nuts, which she places into a bowl in her lap. She talks quietly as she shells the nuts. 'We used to get 1,800 shillings ($1.38) for one kilo.' She puts down the bowl for a moment so that she can extend her long index finger upward to ensure I'm paying attention. Then, through a broad smile, her voice raises an octave. 'But now we sell the same coffee for 4,000 shillings ($3.14) to our new buyers.' Of course her new buyers are Dave and Ian.

I wonder if she thinks that her new buyers have suddenly gone crazy. 'No! They are not crazy!' She laughs a loud happy laugh. 'Now with the sorting shed and the milling we do we are able to produce higher quality. We have told the people in the village that we can only sell good-quality coffee. We want to work harder so that the quality of the coffee will match the price.'

Despite the fact that their cooperative had ethical certification and that coffee prices are at historic highs, the farmers in Orera were receiving a paltry $1.38 per kilo. The reason is that so much of what was going into the cooperative was getting swallowed up in administrative costs, including wages paid to the headmen. Remember that, according to Dave and Ian, for every $100 that goes to the KNCU, as much as $30 or $40 can go to the elders.

The KNCU has over 100,000 members and they are very powerful. 'They also have massive overheads,' says Bente. 'They have offices and employees who need to be paid.' The cooperative is certified and audited by various ethical certification organisations so it can charge an ethical premium for their coffee if they sell it in Europe or the United States to a major company like Kraft Foods or Sainsbury's. But the actual amount going to the villagers was only half of what they found they could get by selling it directly without any certification to Dave and Ian. In this case, being part of the certified cooperative isn't in the best interests of the villagers.

Many of the ethical labelling organisations have prioritised a model whereby farmers are bound to work within the cooperative as a means to best serve their interests. The cooperative is then encouraged to sell to the big buyers on their behalf. The logic is that together they have greater leverage over prices. In fact, the Orera experience shows this to be a fallacy. On their own, the villagers of Orera were able to achieve a much higher price by dealing directly with a smaller high-value Western company.

This is why Bente thinks it is vital that people look beyond certification when they choose where to buy their coffee or tea, or any other product for that matter, and why, despite the premiums on offer, the work with villagers needs a more hands-on approach. 'Even for farms like mine, the only future is with small companies because big companies will always push you on price. Sure, they may pay a premium for certification, but with all the things I am doing here, we can't live on that.'

Although Bente has gone through the rigorous process of registering her own farm for various ethical certificates, she certainly doesn't see it as a money-spinner. In fact it amounts to only a few cents on each kilo if the customer requires it, and so it hardly pays for itself. 'I don't do it for the bloody premium. I'm doing all this anyway. I don't keep a budget and it costs so much more than the premium anyway – not to mention my time.'

Bente even seems a little resentful that she has to spend her time helping the villages like this. Remember, she gives US$45,000 every year to the Primary Cooperative for the lease here. 'To me that should do the trick and I shouldn't have to do any more. The cooperative should use that money to do what they are supposed to do.' She shakes her head and looks down to where she is kicking the dirt below. The fact is that neither her money nor the money paid to the KNCU via the social premium has built the stoves in the village or the sorting shed or any of the number of other initiatives Bente has started. It has taken her a few years here to learn that her sense of responsibility is not always shared.

In fact, Bente says that the KNCU are even a little annoyed that the villagers are now taking their business elsewhere. She denies that this is her fault. The buyers who come to see her farm have merely shown interest in seeing what was being grown in the neighbouring villages and then liked what they saw. But the KNCU are beginning to see Bente as a threat to their own interests.

It was Bente who encouraged the village to reinvest some of their profits into the materials needed to build a separate sorting area for washing and drying their beans. To get their coffee up to a standard to sell independently of the cooperative, they would have to club together and work hard, while she would also have to invest a lot of her own time into training them to use it.

'I see that I have the benefit of information from other farmers, traders and the Internet and I see it as my responsibility to share the know-how. Of course I had to learn my own stuff first. When I decided to start a farm I needed to learn how to do it. Only now can I teach others.' Because the villages are on Bente's borders, they often face the same environmental issues, which means she understands exactly what help they need. 'Whenever they're having a problem, I'm having a problem,' she smiles ruefully.

The village sorting shed now collects coffee from 74 different smallholders. They share the work washing and sorting the coffee and then divvy up the price. It is an independent cooperative operating outside of the Primary Cooperative. If any farmer brings bad coffee to the sorting shed they are sent away. The village has learned that they can't afford to take the risk of damaging their reputation by allowing any poor-quality coffee to get mixed in with the rest.

And that's where the opportunity comes in for UK sellers. They have a product that they can market on two fronts. First, it's good enough quality to sell into the top end of the single estate coffee market where the prices are enough to generate genuine market-driven premiums for the farmers that can be sustained as long as they keep the quality high. And second, they can reassure their customers that they are passing this benefit directly to the farmers and thereby ensuring that there will be more coffee next year and the year after.

It is hard for the villagers to understand why anyone would pay more for the coffee than they have to. Frida points out that their new buyers are good businessmen, so 'They must have their reason. Nobody can work for free,' she says confidently. 'Everybody must have a profit.' This belies the sense of pride that the villagers of Orera have in the improvements that they have made. They understand that they get paid more for better quality but the rationale for an ethical premium paid by Dave and Ian is lost on them. I ask Frida and the other ladies to imagine that one day they go to the market where a kilo of tomatoes normally costs $1 but notice that there is another trader selling tomatoes for only 50 cents. When they ask the trader why his tomatoes are so cheap, he says it is because he beat up the farmer and stole his tomatoes. Now I ask Frida, 'Which tomatoes would you buy?' She pauses to discuss this conundrum with the others, and finally she says, 'I would be tempted to buy the cheaper ones. But I would not because I would be worried it was a trap and that as soon as I had bought them, a policeman would arrest me.'

It seems that Bente is not the only one being ethical for all the 'wrong' reasons. Back in London, at the other end of the supply chain, another woman is making quite a name for herself as an ethical supplier, this time of African tea.

'Let's be clear, I didn't get into this business because I wanted to be ethical. It was because I was passionate about tea.' Henrietta Lovel is an eccentric character. I would say that she seems a little like a character from a novel, but in fact she actually is a character from a novel. Alexander McCall Smith immortalised her when he featured her in his book *Corduroy Mansions*. His central character meets an 'elegant dark-haired woman' whom he calls 'the tea lady'.

Henrietta met Alexander at a tasting session she had organised to market a new addition to her range of rare teas. The Rare Tea Company is an enterprise she set up in 2004 to bring her passion to the palates of British punters. For Henrietta, tea is as important to British culture as wine is to the French. 'Imagine if the French only drank Le Piat d'Or, or in Italy the only coffee you could buy was NESCAFÉ?' This does seem unlikely. But she believes that the loss to British culture that lack of interest in good tea would represent is comparable.

As recently as 1968, only 3 per cent of UK tea drinkers used a tea bag. Yet somewhere along the line, we swapped our teapots for tea bags. Henrietta blames the sort of advertising campaigns used by companies like Yorkshire Tea. 'Tea is not made in Yorkshire by men in little cloth caps.' She rolls her eyes at the thought. In fact, of course, most of our tea comes from India and Africa. And as consumers made the switch to bags, they also opened the door for an international price war.

According to Henrietta, most of the tea entering the UK is now 'poor quality', by which she means produced on the cheap. For Henrietta, tea with genuine flavour needs to be cultivated with care, which takes time and means that ultimately you have to pay more for it. But for the cheap kind of tea most of us drink in tea bags, the price is set on the global market and so the incentive for producers becomes a case of how to produce as much of it as possible – only higher volumes can deliver higher profits. Such a cut-throat approach has often meant that Third World producers have had to sell below the cost of production. 'It's ridiculous that you could produce anything for that much,' says Henrietta.

The history behind our collective shift away from what

Henrietta calls 'quality teas' is fundamental to her efforts. She says it is down to rationing during the Second World War; we began to forget about what we used to drink and gradually became hooked on the cheap stuff, with its distinctive tannin-heavy flavour.

Initially Henrietta was importing tea exclusively from China, the world's number one producer and consumer of tea. Proportionally, the Chinese spend as much of their income on tea as we do on alcohol. In China a good tea will be so highly sought after that the farmer sets the price with confidence because he knows that he will get it. 'There's no concept of fair trade or anything like that there,' says Henrietta, who has made many trips out to see where her Chinese tea is produced. 'If I didn't pay the price my farmer set, then he'd simply sell it elsewhere.' And one of the ironies of so many young people migrating to the cities in China is that picking tea back home has become a well-paid job. The industry is now dominated by the older generation, particularly women, who earn well because their skills and experience are in short supply. 'I know that from what I can see, no one there is being exploited. It's more like an old mothers' meeting.'

Henrietta says that the idea of tea pickers being exploited didn't even enter her head until she went to Africa. What brought her to Africa was that in 2009 *Time* magazine ran a feature on her – the curious English lady who was trying to 'de-bag' Britain. Inevitably the exposure meant that the name Rare Tea Company travelled quickly around the industry and several producers came out of the woodwork to make contact. Then one day a shoebox covered in African stamps was delivered to her door. 'It was literally a box full of tea, with a letter from a man in Malawi called Alexander who asked me if I'd try it.' Of course the tea was exquisite but what was particularly unusual was that it was a black tea – exactly what she'd been looking for. 'I felt so stupid. I'd overlooked a whole continent as somewhere that only produced low-quality tea for the mass market.' She got straight on a plane.

Malawi wasn't the first trip that Henrietta had made looking for a black tea to add to the range. She had previously been to Sri Lanka to look for black teas but wasn't impressed. 'It was my first encounter with mass market traders. Everyone was selling on price and the quality was terrible. And even though many were British-owned, I was concerned about the conditions on the farms.' Henrietta says she realised then that she was more interested in finding a farmer with whom she could build an ongoing relationship rather than someone who would just produce cheaply and offer her a price. Then in Malawi, when she met Alexander, she saw right away that he was someone she would get on with. 'I knew he was a nice man when we shared a joke on day one. There weren't many jokes with my farmer in China,' she smiles.

That first year, Henrietta bought 600 kilograms of tea from Alexander, even though she didn't have a customer for it. The market for gourmet African black tea simply didn't exist yet beyond speciality teashops and top-end restaurants, many of whom Henrietta sells tea to already – including top UK restaurant the Fat Duck. So if she was going to be able to shift all of Alexander's Malawian tea she needed one of the big supermarkets to get on board. Initially they weren't interested. 'I couldn't just ask them to sell an African tea as a gourmet product – they'd laugh at me. I needed to create a market.' This is where the illustrious Scottish novelist came in.

Alexander McCall Smith shares Henrietta's passion for tea and, having been born in southern Africa, he believes passionately that Africa does much more than only produce cheap inferior products. Henrietta went to see him in his home in Edinburgh and explained the background to her tea purchase. The author got it right away. 'He said, "Right, well, we'll call it Lost Malawi," which was great because I'd been struggling for a name. And then he said he'd write some short stories to go in the packaging.' This was the spark she needed and enough to catch the interest of UK supermarket Waitrose who started stocking the tea straight away.

'There was loads of crap quality but ethically certified teas coming out of Africa already,' she says, 'but African products can stand up next to the best in the rest of the world.' And she feels good about the impact that her business is having in Malawi. This year she has already placed an order with Alexander for 4 tonnes, and she is paying ten times more for it than she would be if she was buying the lower-quality tea that he sells on the Fairtrade market. 'Tea is their second biggest export and life expectancy is forty to forty-five years. There's a reason that your tea bags are cheap – even your Fairtrade ones,' she says.

What Henrietta has done is to establish a new market for a quality product from a farmer who would otherwise have produced something for the cheap mass market. Because the price he gets for the tea he sells to Henrietta is dictated by quality, he can invest time in its production, which in turn guarantees him a higher price. The important thing is that the tea is grown, harvested and produced for flavour and not for volume. And that is the source of Henrietta's ethical credentials. She may not be driven by a desire to ensure that a particular ethical logo appears on her product, but her business methods and approach make her seem, to me at least, worthy of one.

Henrietta has achieved what she has despite the fact that it's so hard for smaller companies to get the credit they deserve. She can only dream of getting the exposure from the national press that Cadbury received when they put an ethical logo on their Dairy Milk bar. And Bente works all hours to support her local communities and yet she is seen as the enemy by the cooperative.

And it's not all about the developing world. This year Henrietta found a way to tie her product to an ethical campaign at home that also helps get the message behind her marketing across. Remember that she believes our taste for quality tea was replaced by a love of cheap tea during the lean times of the Second World War.

To get this point across, Henrietta made a short film with the RAF to commemorate 70 years since the Battle of Britain and let out a rallying cry to Britain's tea drinkers to rediscover the tea that our grandparents drank. To charm the old pilots, she specially prepared a pot of old-school tea that she thought would most closely resemble the tea that they had drunk before rationing and the war.

Using some of her Malawian leaves, she produced a tea which they liked so much it gave her an idea. She launched a new old-style tea packaged with the red and blue symbol of the RAF on it that promised to donate 10 per cent of the retail price to a relief fund for Air Force veterans – the RAF Association Wings Appeal. You might have thought that given its doubly ethical credentials, her usual retailer would have jumped at the opportunity to stock it. You'd be wrong.

'It was still early in our relationship,' says Henrietta, 'and maybe it was a bit much to ask them to stock another black tea so soon.' The RAF were keen for Henrietta to get the new tea to as many people as possible – a bigger retailer was what they wanted. 'But it's incredibly difficult for a small company to even get a meeting with a supermarket buyer, let alone convince them to stock your product. You have to be inventive.'

Henrietta decided on Sainsbury's as her ideal choice as they had national reach and a good reputation for quality. But to convince them to try out what she was selling, she turned to unorthodox means. 'I left a message for the head of grocery saying I needed to see him but it was "top secret". I couldn't divulge any details over the phone.' She had clearly picked up a trick or two from her Air Force chums. She arrived on the day with a Squadron Leader in full uniform. 'It's very difficult to say no to a man who has just arrived back from Afghanistan.' Now she had their attention.

What Henrietta says is hard in the current market is to develop a good British brand with solid ethical credentials. But she believes it is fundamentally important that one needs the other. 'You can't just give them a story without the quality. You need to give them both.' She firmly believes that the story might draw a customer in the first time but then it's the quality of the product that will keep them coming back.

Sainsbury's agreed to stock her RAF tea, but supermarkets only agree to sell products, not to buy them. Meanwhile farmers need to be paid up front, so the risk has to be borne by Henrietta. She has put a down payment on what she hopes will be enough to supply tea for the next 12 months. 'I've risked my shirt on this,' she says. So far, at the time of writing, the RAF tea has only been on the shelves for a couple of months so it's too early to say how successful it will be. Henrietta has done as much as she can. Let's hope it's enough, for the Malawian farmer's sake as well as her own.

At the moment, you could reasonably argue that this is all small-scale stuff. The kind of tea that Henrietta sells and coffee that Dave and Ian have begun buying from Orera village is in the niche sector. And Bente admits that she now sees her future more with small companies operating in these niche markets than with the big corporates that cater for the mass market.

Because over 90 per cent of tea is bought as a commodity for a price set by the market with little or no accounting for quality, there's little opportunity for smaller high-quality producers to try to break in, especially in the context of Malawian tea, which is at the bottom end of even the African scale. So as things stand, ethical producers and sellers who want the bigger margins associated with higher-quality produce must compete in the other 10 per cent of the market.

However, the fact that two businesses like Ethical Addictions and the Rare Tea Company exist at all in a fiendishly competitive marketplace shows that such enterprises can make economic sense. Henrietta has even shown that with some persistence it is possible to penetrate the all-important supermarkets. Just having her products on the shelves of Sainsbury's and Waitrose should be cause for celebration.

It is important to recognise the potential power these business models could have to shift our perceptions and our buying patterns. After all, Green & Black's started as a niche business competing with such giants as Cadbury, and now its products are mainstream to such an extent that first Cadbury and then Kraft Foods actually wanted to take them over.

What's more, having taken them over, their new corporate parents say that they aim to continue to operate with the same ethical principles in mind. And remember Green & Black's was already operating with the highest ethical principles, long before it became Fairtrade accredited.

Above all, these two success stories, when contrasted with the experiences in various parts of the world, make a very convincing argument for the superiority of cleverly constructed local solutions over top-down answers provided by ethical organisations, whether concerned with trade or the politics of trade.

You might argue that this is fine when dealing in niche markets and that, while it might help the 10 per cent who are lucky enough to benefit from higher revenues in the quality market, it doesn't necessarily offer much to the other 90 per cent. But what needs to be addressed is whether the local approach can be rolled out so that it works for big manufacturing industries as well.

The question that remained in my mind after my encounters with Bente and Henrietta was not, therefore, whether carefully honed local solutions work – they clearly do; it was whether they can be applied successfully on a larger scale. I have to confess that I felt a bit dubious. That is, until I came across a mention of a company named Olam operating in Côte d'Ivoire. That set me off on the final leg of my journey.

8

Cottoning on

Côte d'Ivoire: the rebel north

'It does us no good to have poor and hungry farmers'

I had intended to arrive in Côte d'Ivoire a month earlier, but my trip had to be delayed when the president ordered the army to close all the country's borders after recent presidential elections designed to unite this divided country – seven years after a bloody civil war – backfired. As I write, the incumbent president, Laurent Gbagbo, continues to hang on to power despite losing the election. The man widely credited with securing more votes is effectively under house arrest in the country's largest city, Abidjan, under the protection of the UN. In the past month hundreds have been killed and thousands have fled as violence has slowly escalated.

Unable to delay any longer, I have decided to come anyway and avoid the epicentre of the violence by taking the long way round via Burkina Faso, which borders to the north. This means that I have to make a 650-kilometre trip by road, heading south along the main road connecting the centre of the continent with the west coast, all the while with the hot harmattan wind at my back. The wind carries with it a dust cloud from the Sahara that sits low in the sky like a fog. All along the route we pass villages, mostly small collections of mud huts built close to the road, whose inhabitants go about their business with their shirts pulled up to cover their mouths and noses. Despite the dust, the temperature outside is over 30 degrees. The combination of the two is what creates the perfect dry, arid atmosphere needed to grow one of this region's principal cash crops: cotton.

At the Côte d'Ivoire border I wait for the guard to leaf through my passport. A number of buses loaded up with Burkinabes pass through the barrier heading in the opposite direction. The threat of further violence in Côte d'Ivoire has been enough, it seems, to encourage them to return home. Last time violence like this erupted in Côte d'Ivoire, it turned to civil war. Eventually the border guard locates my visa and reaches for the stamp that will allow me entry. This soldier is remarkably chatty. 'We need one president,' he says. He points the end of the stamp at me as though to emphasise that this is a key piece of information. 'Two presidents for one country is like a dream.'

'You mean a nightmare?' I ask.

'Yes,' he says, nodding. 'That's right, it is a nightmare.' With a sad smile, he hands back my documents and motions with his long arm that I am free to pass through the barrier and into what is known as the 'rebel zone' – the part of northern Côte d'Ivoire that has been under the control of rebel forces since the hostilities of the early 2000s. The events of the past few years have become known in Côte d'Ivoire simply as *la Crise*.

I have chosen to come to Côte d'Ivoire because its problems so closely resemble those of some of the other countries I've visited over the past few months. Like Nicaragua, it is a country that has experienced recent civil war. Like Tanzania – and much of Africa – it faces serious environmental and social problems. Like the Democratic Republic of Congo and Afghanistan, it currently faces an appalling political crisis and the everyday dangers posed by rebel groups. And like Laos, it is a country that is trying to develop a very poor agrarian society with foreign investment. Yet I have heard that Côte d'Ivoire also bears witness to business operating in an ethically minded, socially responsible, sustainable and profitable way – and on a large scale: the cotton industry.

Further down the road from the border I pass a donkey pulling a cart on which there are four tall wooden posts standing vertically at each corner like a large upside-down table. Squeezed in between the posts is what looks like the most enormous ball of cotton wool I've ever seen, and as the donkey edges slowly down the bumpy road it seems the cotton will topple off into the dust with every step. This is a typical scene in the West African cotton-growing region, and it typifies the difficulty faced by Ivorian farmers when producing cotton.

Cotton, by its very nature, is a difficult crop to transport. A farmer with a cart like this can transport around 200–300 kilograms only a short distance. But before cotton can be exported to the countries in the African subcontinent and in South East Asia where it is spun, it first needs to be processed to remove the seeds buried within its fibres and the useless plant debris that gets mixed in at picking time. To do that, the cotton needs to be run through a factory known as a gin.

At the time of the civil war in 2002–4 there were ten gins in Côte d'Ivoire, but following the war years they were all gradually run down into a state of disrepair, and the company responsible for those in the north-east of the country went bankrupt in 2006. It was then that the government, having no money itself to repair them, decided to put the region's cotton gins up for tender. The largest of them was bought by the world's number one trader and spinner of cotton lint – Olam.

Olam are responsible for the supply and management of 20 different agricultural products across over 60 countries with a total annual turnover of $10 billion. They specialise in the distribution not just of cotton but also of coffee and chocolate. The company is listed on the Singapore stock exchange where the global head-quarters are located and their end customers include many high-street brands, such as Marks and Spencer and Gap.

Within Côte d'Ivoire, Olam's major commercial interests have traditionally been the supply and distribution of cocoa; the move into cotton was a more recent strategic choice. Their decision to buy an Ivorian cotton gin was part of a major (multimillion-dollar) investment in the country's future as a player in the cotton industry and represents a substantial financial risk. It also offers a potential lifeline to this particular region's farmers, as there isn't another gin to be found for over 100 kilometres.

Côte d'Ivoire is a small player on the world stage compared to the mega producers in the United States. Cotton farming in the north and south of the globe couldn't be more different. In the US the industry consists of fewer than 25,000 farmers operating heavily irrigated, mechanised farms of over 230 hectares each, while Africa's 2.5 million farmers mostly use oxen to work their single-hectare fields and can only pray that the rain will come to water their crops. A US farmer will be disappointed to produce less than 215 tonnes of lint in a year, while the average African farmer would be delighted to end up with 1 or 2 tonnes. But if you take all those 2.5 million African farmers together, the total amount of cotton they produce becomes significant enough to bother about – nearly 20 per cent of global cotton exports.

The individual responsible for the running of Olam's cotton operations in Côte d'Ivoire is Julie Greene, a tall and elegant-looking 30-year-old American expat who has been resident on the African continent for seven years. She began her African experience as an NGO worker, during which time, she says, she built her fair share of village schools and water pumps. Julie joined Olam two years ago, having become frustrated at the lack of progress she felt she was making within communities with an NGO. 'I suspected that I could get more done through the commercial sector,' she says. And so she left Africa, got an MBA in Geneva and returned a year later to take the job with Olam in Côte d'Ivoire. She feels that the decision was the right one. 'For sure, I think it was the right move because I feel I'm making much more of a difference this way.'

The first challenge was to get the old gin up off its knees and back into production. The industrial process of ginning requires several large machines to separate the cotton seed from the lint fibres used in garment production, so it was essential to invest in acquiring and restoring the gin in Oungaloudougou. Oungalou, as it is known to the locals, is a dirty town built at a crossroads in the heart of Western Africa. There's no industry in town except the cotton gin, and although each of its four roads will take you directly to the respective capitals of Côte d'Ivoire, Burkina, Ghana and Mali, they are all at least 650 kilometres away, so you can't expect to reach any of them quickly. Oungalou town is a cotton town, and whether it's in the small stalls that sell espresso in the morning or the carts that hawk street-food at dusk, all the talk is about cotton.

In the first year after Olam took over, the plant managed to get back up to 70 per cent of its design capability – not bad for a bunch of machines built in 1975 and barely serviced for the previous ten years. But this year it has gone one better and now Julie is overseeing the processing of 200 tonnes of raw cotton every day. At that volume, the plant is running at full capacity.

Julie's initial challenge at the gin was more than simply maximising production volumes. There was considerable work to be done just to make the factory a safe place to work. Siaka, a 40-year-old Oungaloun, is the factory's senior electrician; he has worked there all his life and now lives on the site with his family. He says he was concerned for a long time about safety shortcomings in the factory, but getting anything done about it was hard. Under the previous management he went 11 months without even being paid, so he says there wasn't much hope of getting funding for basic safety improvements. But since the new management arrived, he says, things have been much easier. On a tour of the gin he points up to the cables that run across in safety cages. 'These are all new,' he says proudly. 'Before, they just hung uncovered. It was very dangerous.' Our tour takes in the new transformer, a generator and the water pump that has just been installed to deal with the frequent fires that break out – cotton ginning is a notoriously flammable process, as the fine dry cotton lint passes through hot industrial machinery. Siaka's particular favourite improvement is an enormous new fuse box that guarantees no one is going to get electrocuted to death. 'I am much happier with the situation now,' he observes with a little nod before double-checking that I've understood. 'Before it was very dangerous.'

Mamadou, the factory foreman, agrees. Having worked in the industry since 1979, he says he has seen remarkable improvements in the conditions in this factory since Olam's arrival. 'Even basic safety equipment like gloves, masks and safety glasses are always available here. In the factory I used to work at, the workers were given one set of safety equipment every year only. If you broke it then the bosses said, "Too bad." You didn't get another one.' It strikes me how much we complain these days in the West about our health and safety obsessed culture, and yet it has been exported to create such a profound change here in West Africa.

One thing that is unique about what Olam are doing in Côte d'Ivoire is the way they are extending their attention right to the end of the supply chain. Julie says that what excited her so much about taking this job was the opportunity it gave her to look for ways in which to align corporate business interests with developmental needs in the region; that doesn't just mean factory workers but also the farmers who supply the cotton. What is also unique about all this is that it is happening within a conflict zone; it's one thing modernising a run-down factory but quite another to keep it operational in an area being run by rebel militia.

When I first thought about writing this book, I hadn't envisaged that it would be necessary to spend so much time talking to soldiers and combatants, but I am once again on my way to do just that. I want to understand what companies and farmers are up against in Côte d'Ivoire as they try to make their living. As I have seen on other legs of this journey, in countries where there is conflict, when the men with guns are a part of life they cannot be ignored; they have to be factored in. So, again, I'm sitting down to talk with a man who has taken up arms and engaged in bloody combat. Koffi (not his real name) is a middle-ranking officer in the Forces Nouvelles, who have controlled the northern region of Côte d'Ivoire since 2002 and remain defiantly resistant to one of the country's two presidents, Laurent Gbagbo.

Much of the media coverage of the current phase of *la Crise* has portrayed the conflict in Côte d'Ivoire as a battle between the largely Muslim north and the Christian south. Koffi is quick to explain that this is a nonsense: not only is he in fact originally from the south but he is also a Buddhist. The Forces Nouvelles, he explains, is like most of Côte d'Ivoire in that it is made up of a mixture of religions and cultures. The cause is not a religiously motivated one, he insists, but one based on strong differences in ideology. 'We are fighting for democracy against tyranny and intolerance.'

Koffi is a tall, strong-looking man in his early 30s. He explains his own reasons for joining the Forces Nouvelles with a passionate intensity; all the while his bright eyes do not stray from mine even for a second. Koffi says that he moved from the south to the north as a teenager to further his education, at which time he was billeted with a host family. He lived with his adopted family for four years; he still refers to them as his brothers and sisters. It was while travelling with his 'brother' in 2000 that he came face to face with a type of behaviour he did not recognise as Ivorian. 'Our bus was stopped and we were told to get out and show our papers,' he recalls. 'When they saw my southern name they let me pass, but my brother, because he had a northern name, was taken away by the police.' Koffi says that his eyes were opened to what was happening to his country and he felt compelled to do something about it. 'I had to take up arms because that was the only way to be heard.'

Within two years of Koffi signing up, the Forces Nouvelles lauched a *coup d'état*, which plunged Côte d'Ivoire into war. Koffi fought in the north-east of the country against a mixture of his own countrymen and Liberian mercenaries until 2004, when the Forces Nouvelles conceded and a peace accord was signed by both sides promising nationwide democratic elections. The Forces Nouvelles retreated to the north of the country but had to wait six years for elections that eventually happened in December 2010. 'We had already begun to arrange what we were going to do next,' Koffi says, shaking his head and sucking his teeth in frustration. 'I already had my papers ready so that I could join the police; others will join the national army. If Gbagbo accepts the result of the elections then we are all ready to put down our arms and reunite as one country. All we wish for is that our country can once again function normally.'

As long as President Gbagbo hangs on to power in Côte d'Ivoire, however, Côte d'Ivoire does not function 'normally'. Gbagbo still controls the south and the Forces Nouvelles continue with their operations in the north with a police force, a gendarmerie and an army – all of which cost money. Unlike in the Congo, this militia operates in a very professional fashion. Taxes are imposed on local businesses, of which Olam are one of the largest. The rebel zone is landlocked and therefore cut off from the southern ports, so the Forces Nouvelles also tax goods moving in and out of the region. 'Cotton is of course important to us,' says Koffi, 'but cotton is important to the Ivorian people so that is why we support the cotton industry.'

It may not always feel like support to Julie. Olam have to pay their official taxes to the government in Abidjan as well as to the Forces Nouvelles. But the two sides have at least 'thrashed out' an agreement that allows business to continue and people to live peacefully. For example, the rate at which each shipment of cotton will be taxed has been mutually agreed for the next 12 months. It is testament to their negotiation skills and their determination that Olam are able to walk the fine line needed to keep business alive. In many other countries experiencing conflict like this, the big international company would have long ago pulled out. Of course that would have left the farmers with little or no way to make a living.

*

Our Pajero jeep bumps along the dirt road towards Sandokaha village, 60 kilometres from the factory in Oungaloudougou. Other than the lush green mango and cashew trees, the fields either side of the road are brown and stripped bare as far as the eye can see. It is as though a swarm of locusts has passed through in the night. In the distance a snow-white pile of cotton the size of the average Western family car gives away the true story. I have arrived just as the picking season is coming to an end. In total, Olam's range covers around 400,000 hectares of northern Côte d'Ivoire. This is no small-scale niche market operation.

Mid-morning we arrive in Sandokaha village. The village presents a typical African rural scene: 20 or so mud huts with thatched roofs arranged around a central clearing. The women of the village are busily preparing pots of water in which to fix lunch, small children draped over their shoulders or in a few cases literally hanging from their breasts. The men are languishing under the shade of a large mango tree in the centre of the village. With cotton picking now over and next season's planting not due to start for another month or three at least, this is an easy time for the farmers.

Daoda, the village head, invites me to join him in the shade of the tree and we begin to chat with the other farmers. They are mostly men in their 30s, except for one softly spoken man with a small greying beard who tells me that his name is Soro and he is the village's oldest working farmer at the ripe old age of 53. Daoda and Soro are happy because this year the harvest has been good, prices are high and they are already being paid.

'We have twenty-one farmers in this village, and in all we planted thirty-five hectares of cotton this year,' says Daoda. 'I have increased my cultivation to nine hectares. And I estimate over ten tonnes of cotton.' This puts Daoda in the category of star farmer, that is one with a yield of over 1,100 kilograms per hectare. As a reward for the high yield he has achieved this year, next year he will automatically be able to get additional credit from Olam's *crédit étoile* scheme. Olam provide all their farmers with free seeds and subsidised fertilisers and pesticides, but last year Olam also gave out over $40,000 in interest-free loans to their star farmers.

Daoda and Soro can remember when things were not so good. During the years leading up to the war, the owners of the gin sent in trucks to take away the cotton but payments were always delayed. 'At first it was a month or two late, but eventually they stopped paying altogether,' says Soro. 'In the end we were not paid for two years. It was a bad time.' Daoda says that he almost gave up growing cotton altogether. In immediate terms, he reduced the area of cotton under cultivation to almost nothing. Then after the war the company went bust and the government had to appoint an administrator to run the gin while they sought a new buyer. Enter Olam. Since then, both men say that things have been improving. Daoda says that what has made the farmers most happy is that Olam always pay on time. He also points out that they provide the things the farmers need to grow good-quality cotton: seeds, fertilisers and pesticides – what they call 'inputs'.

I wonder how different these vital inputs are from what he used to get. Both farmers share a look before they burst out laughing. Then Daoda reaches down to touch the red earth below him and looks back up towards me. 'It is like the difference between the earth and the sky,' he says. He has no doubt that Olam are the first company in a long time to give him what he needs to do his job properly.

Daoda can remember when the region first began growing cotton in the late 1970s. As he tells me his story, he reminds me of Borsai, the rubber farmer in Laos who first brought rubber plants back from China. Daoda describes how all the African farmers were suspicious at first but slowly they came round to the idea of the new crop. Things went well back then and Daoda says that by the early 1990s everyone was growing cotton. Things were good. 'People were tranquil and there was real social cohesion,' he says. 'But the war destroyed it all. That's gone now.' Of course Laos hasn't suffered a recent civil war as Côte d'Ivoire has, and I'm aware of the danger of oversimplifying the comparison, but it does seem to me that, when you compare Olam's operation here to that of the Chinese Ruifeng Rubber company in Laos, Daoda and Soro are doing a lot better than could so easily be the case.

Another comparison comes to mind when Soro explains how *la Crise* is affecting the village's trading options. 'Since the recent problems, the trucks have not been able to take our maize to the markets in the south,' he says. 'So the only crop we can trade is cotton because Olam come here to collect it.' In Afghanistan I had heard similar complaints from opium farmers who were often reluctant to switch to growing wheat because of the logistical problems involved in moving it to market through militarised checkpoints. They pointed out that when mafia-type groups wanted to buy, at least they came directly to the farm gate to collect. Opium in Afghanistan and cotton in Côte d'Ivoire are scarcely comparable, but it does seem that many of the problems faced by the rural poor are the same the world over.

Buying the gin in Oungalou put Olam in the driving seat. Cotton is a unique crop in that the final product sold by the farmer to the gin contains not just the lint but also the seed cotton, which means that, unlike wheat or maize, the farmer doesn't retain any seeds for next year's crop. The strategic importance of being the gin owner is that in a cotton-growing community the ginner controls the seed going back to the farmer. That has allowed Olam not only to control the variety of cotton being grown but also to monitor closely the yields being returned each year. Julie explains the rationale. 'It means we have the power to issue farmers with better-quality seeds, which we do for free because it means they only use our seeds and [it] reduces the risk to us of getting any contamination in our supply chain.' And of course it means more chance for the farmers to produce higher-quality product, too, for which Olam are happy to pay a higher price.

Olam are also encouraging the farmers to supply their cotton with the best conditions to grow. One scheme has been to pre-finance pesticides and fertilisers – again interest-free so that they don't have to incur these costs up front. The problem that most Third World farmers have is that they don't have the means to invest in the things that would improve the quality of their product. Olam try to take that headache away from their cotton farmers. The farmers pay back the costs from their profits at the end of the process and then get to pocket the extra profits.

Daoda says that if Olam had not stepped in to save the gin, things would have been grim indeed. 'Without cotton, life would be very hard here. If there was no cotton to sell, it would be a catastrophe – there would be hunger and famine.' But there isn't hunger here in Sandokaha village. On the contrary, things here are good. Daoda shows me three new silos that the villagers have built in the centre of the village; one is filled to the brim with rice and two with maize. This is the first time the village has had so much food in a long time. In fact, Daoda says they even have food left over from last year.

In a corner of the village there are several large piles of dried maize. 'This is what is left over from last year's crop,' says Daoda, 'but now insects are damaging it.' He peels back the sheath to reveal a kernel riddled with black holes and explains that there is a chemical that would protect maize identified for long-term storage and prevent this happening again next year. Julie is interested right away. 'That's something we could look into pre-financing,' she says. It strikes me that, just as with Bente in Tanzania, the very fact that Julie is here full-time allows her to spot opportunities and to support initiatives that can have profound effects. Of course the difference here is that if Julie gives the go-ahead it will affect a very large number of people indeed: 5,000 farmers and their families means that 30,000 will benefit. 'It's a massive responsibility,' she laughs a little nervously, 'when you realise how many lives are affected by the decisions you make.'

What helps Julie make those decisions, however, is her strong commercial sense. 'I believe that these kinds of initiatives are only worth it if they're sustainable,' she says. 'And they're only sustainable if they're profitable.'

Take her decision to offer farmers fertiliser not just for their cotton but also for their maize fields, for example. Olam has no commercial interest in maize production, but they realised that if they gave farmers four bags of fertiliser to put on their cotton, then inevitably one bag would end up on the maize field. 'Better to just provide an extra bag,' says Julie. 'That way they still put enough fertiliser on the cotton to ensure we get the good-quality supply we need.' For the cost of an extra bag of fertiliser she worked out that the extra yield made commercial sense. And of course the farmers benefited. 'It does us no good to have poor and hungry farmers.'

But it's not always a case of being the friendly boss. Julie has to be pragmatic about what is necessary to get the best out of the farmers. She often has to make much harder decisions. Many have asked her why Olam don't help them to mechanise their farms: why not, for instance, send tractors out to turn over the fields after planting time? Julie, however, doesn't see this as necessarily the best way to develop the industry. Trying to farm single-hectare plots with a tractor is not always that practical. Moreover, there have been plenty of schemes in the past where farmers have done themselves out of better yields because they have been promised the loan of a tractor and then wasted time sitting around waiting for it to arrive before planting too late, so instead Olam are issuing oxen to farmers as a kind of capital loan package. A pair of working oxen can cultivate 5 hectares. The key with cotton is to get the seed in the ground as soon after the start of the rainy season as possible. Julie says it's a simple equation: 'Unless they can drastically increase their yields then it's simply not worth it.'

Encouraging farmers to use oxen may seem a retrograde move for a major corporation, but the key for Olam is to make sure that they get the best possible return from the 25,000 hectares' worth of seeds they have given out. To do that they need to make sure the seeds get put in the ground as early as possible, and the best way to achieve that is to encourage farmer self-sufficiency.

Of course it isn't practical to deal with 5,000 farmers individually. Traditionally, the farmers in Côte d'Ivoire are organised into cooperatives. Julie says that she sees working with them as a 'necessary headache' because, while they can be useful in coordinating the distribution of key tools, fertiliser and so on and offsetting some of the risk, they can be very corrupt. The heads of the cooperatives get paid in two ways from the cotton process. First they put a 'tax' of around 2 per cent on the cotton by under-reporting to their own farmers the total weight delivered. 'In ninety-eight per cent of cases the weight we pay the cooperative is more than they have reported to the farmers,' says Julie. Of course, it is the heads who pocket the difference.

In addition, Olam pay every cooperative what you might call a 'social premium' of 7.3 CFA francs per kilo (3.5 per cent), intended to go back to the cooperative to fund community projects. But the money rarely makes its way back to the farmers. 'The managers of the big cooperatives see it as a personal enterprise. First there are the ones who skim off the top by selling the inputs; that's the worst type. The less bad type are the ones who say, "If I have more farmers then all of that end-of-year bonus, I get to pocket." I know the leader of one cooperative who drives around in a Mercedes even though his cooperative is in debt.'

But dealing with these individuals, she says, is unavoidable. Cotton prices on the global markets are at a record high this year and so Olam are hungry for as much supply as possible. That means that they need the cooperatives' business, even if they disapprove of how the leaders are operating; they can't afford to challenge them in a way that turns them away to their competitors.

Julie says that she has to be pragmatic; she realises that the system won't work unless the leader gets some extra profit. At the same time she wants to represent the farmers' interests. It's a fine line she has to walk. 'I have to try to ensure that our farmers get cheated as little as possible while accepting that some amount of extra profit has to go to the leaders. You just don't want it to be excessive.' She says that ideally the cooperatives would be open with their own farmers about the amounts involved. 'They'd draw a reasonable salary but leave enough over to pay for some sort of community projects. But try being transparent when everyone is illiterate . . .'

This all strikes me as remarkably similar to what I had seen in Orera village in Tanzania. Like Bente, Julie needs to be careful not to get involved in the internal politics of the big cooperatives. Just as Bente had described to me in Kilimanjaro, the leaders of the big cooperatives in Côte d'Ivoire can get easily upset if they think that the outsider is meddling with their own private business interests. Julie says that even in cases here when smaller villages have realised that they're getting ripped off by their own leaders and so have tried to break away and secure a better deal for themselves, it's the Westerner who has tended to get the blame: 'The leaders accuse us of trying to break up the cooperatives even when we are careful not to get involved.'

Julie says she doesn't believe that things have always been like this in Côte d'Ivoire. 'Everyone talks about how these people used to be so proud, hardworking and honest, but over the past ten to fifteen years, between the war and the rebellion, that culture has been totally destroyed. Now all the stealing and cheating has come through and that has just infected the culture.' The challenge is to turn that culture around. One way would be to incentivise farmers who produce the best cotton by grading prices to reflect different qualities. The government, however, currently prohibits such behaviour. Côte d'Ivoire cotton companies only recognise two standards of cotton quality, and the price for each is fixed by the government to ensure that the farmers receive a fair deal. Olam try to get around this by offering prizes to the farmers returning the highest yields. So far, Julie says, the competition is bringing out the best in them.

Some evidence of Olam's longer-term ambition to empower the farmers to help themselves can be seen in villages such as Sandokaha. With a little encouragement, the village have clubbed together to renovate one of their older unused buildings into a potential schoolroom. Nobody in the village asked for a literacy programme, but Olam see helping farmers in this way as something that will help them, too, in the long run. The aim is to try to teach the farmers basic literacy and numeracy skills. Olam said that if they could see evidence that the village were investing in a school building then they would stump up the cash to provide the training for the teacher. There's only been one little glitch. 'We said they had to find someone who had at least completed high school,' says Julie, but that's proved harder than she expected. 'When I came here at first I expected to find seventy or eighty per cent illiteracy. But among the farmers it's more like ninety-seven or ninety-eight per cent. And around thirty per cent can't even count to five.' That's a serious worry for a company who are trying to increase transparency, never mind educating them about how to increase yields. 'You can forget trying to talk to people in terms of a thirty per cent increase in yield if they do X, Y, Z when they can't even count how many bags of fertiliser they've used,' she points out. But today the village have stepped up to the mark. They have seized the mettle and the school building has been adorned with a brand new blackboard. Julie sees this as the sign she's been looking for that they are serious. 'I guess we're going to have to find them a teacher.'

A sign of how seriously Olam are taking the idea of corporate social responsibility at corporate level can be seen by where they put their CSR department's offices. From the top floor of one of central London's most desirable addresses, Olam's head of CSR, Chris Brett, can look out of his office window over the Houses of Parliament and along the river Thames. It's a far cry from the cotton fields of West Africa.

Chris is the hub for the programmes Olam run around the world and as soon as I arrive at his office he is keen to start talking me through how the company's Côte d'Ivoire programmes fit in with their overall corporate strategy and how especially proud he is of the Côte d'Ivoire projects. He has a presentation already loaded up on his iPad, and the first slide shows just how rapid the increase in scale of Olam-supported cotton farming has been in the country. The total number of farmers supplying Olam has tripled in two years – hectares under cultivation have reached 20,000 – and what he's most proud about is the steady rise in yields from an average of 600 to nearer 1,000 kilograms per hectare. 'That's the key,' says Chris. 'Better yields buffer farmers from price fluctuations. That's what we're striving to improve all the time.'

Chris says Olam were initially worried about the price tag on the gin in Côte d'Ivoire. At $5 million, it was a big commitment. 'The old cotton gin just wasn't able to run economically any more, and so we knew we had to invest big to completely modernise it.' But keeping a gin running is also expensive, so Olam needed the farmers to play their part and produce enough cotton to make it work. 'We've worked out that we need to be ginning a minimum of 15,000 tonnes of seed cotton to break even. But when we first went into Côte d'Ivoire the total production was less than 9,000.' It's because of Julie and the hard work of her team and the local farmers that the scheme has come good.

In two years Olam have offered 5,000 Ivorian farmers opportunities to return to profitable cotton cultivation. They are already achieving much higher yields and profits than they were even before the war. Chris says that Olam have merely enabled the process; the farmers still had to make the most of the opportunities by putting in the necessary hard work. 'If you depend on other people,' he says, 'you won't go anywhere.'

All this demonstrates how poor rural farming communities can benefit from association with a commercially minded corporate. I think back to what Julie said about providing oxen rather than tractors and can see how, without true commercial insight, it would be easy to assume that mechanisation and new equipment like tractors is what is needed by these communities. Indeed this has often been the strategy followed by NGOs working in the developing world. Olam, however, think about everything that will directly improve profitability: seeds, oxen, soil quality, waste management and a whole range of other processes. 'Our profit comes from our management,' says Chris. 'Adding value through the processing and how we sell it is how we build profits across the supply chain, and our skill is making it all commercially viable.'

Just as Daoda had said to me in the village, Chris in the Olam boardroom says that he sees the arrangement as a partnership between Olam and the farmers, where both sides need to do what they do best to make it profitable all round. 'The last thing we want to do is to pay farmers below the cost of growing [their crops].' Cotton is an annually planted crop, so if it doesn't pay this year few farmers will plant it again next year, and with millions of dollars sunk into it already that's a risk Olam can't afford to take. 'Every time we can help farmers to improve yields, we help to buffer farmers and ourselves from the implications of a fall in prices. For us, it's a business, and we have to make it work.' Farmers living on the edge of subsistence are no good to Chris if a fall in global prices of, say, 10 per cent pushes them over that edge.

Olam's long-term challenge is how to keep scaling up when increasing scale requires considerably more working capital for the farmers. Chris's hope is that, as his farming groups in Côte d'Ivoire prove that they are commercially viable once again, they will be able to develop a credit rating which will allow them to apply for loans from rural banks. This is the key to farmers achieving true self-sufficiency, and is fundamental to the initiative being truly sustainable long-term. 'We will invite a local bank in to get involved with the farmers to lend and we become the guarantor. So the farmers that do well can reinvest. People who were previously thought to be "unbankable" can become investors in their own futures.'

Olam are open about their own interest in these initiatives. Chris says that the company are already generating good profits from cotton being grown in Côte d'Ivoire and that they are particularly keen to develop a cotton production centre outside of the US, Brazil and China, countries that together produce over 70 per cent of the global supply.

Once Olam have ginned the cotton from the farmers, they take it to the spinners who produce cotton fabric for the production of garments. Consequently, the spinners play a key role in the traceability of cotton. The cotton shirt you're wearing now will most likely be made up of several different types of cotton, each grown in a completely different region of the world. This makes the supply chain incredibly complicated. Chris's challenge is to connect his Côte d'Ivoire cotton directly with consumers.

Keen to try to link their customers back to producers, Tesco recently proposed labelling all their cotton garments in such a way as to show exactly where the material is produced. Chris thought it was a great idea, but with seven or eight countries contributing cotton to the final mix he had to point out to them that the label might need to be bigger than the shirt it was attached to. So as things stand the retailer can link back only as far as the spinner, and then companies like Olam link from the spinner to the farmer. Olam would like to be able to sell their ethically produced cotton directly on to the market, but to do so they would have to take more control of the spinning process. If they could do that, they could bridge the link and have an Olam-labelled cotton on the market.

Another route might be to look towards ethical certification for Olam cotton. But Chris thinks that the solution doesn't lie there. Even though Olam work with Fairtrade Foundation and Rainforest Alliance in other industries they manage, such as coffee and cocoa, he doesn't see the same approach working when applied to cotton. 'Many retailers and customers say they want certification because they see it's there for other products so they want it in this one too. But they're actually just parking the problems. They think because it's certified it will be fine.' When customers are asked why they want this, he says their reasons are usually twofold. 'They want it for their marketing and so that they can tick the box that says they've made their contribution to managing their supply chain.'

And often, although retailers say they want more certification on their products, they are reluctant to pick up the tab for the extra certification costs involved. 'We don't want those costs on us, so who's going to pay them? The farmer?' Chris feels as though sometimes his job is to negotiate on behalf of the farmers to protect them.

And that's not all. Chris has more fundamental doubt about the concept of certification. 'Certification is still very niche; it isn't really mainstream.' And therein lies the limitation to making the big difference that Chris is looking for. 'If you produce for niche markets, you're not really solving the bigger problem.' Chris would rather that Olam became synonymous with sustainability and ethical practices in its own right.

By lending money to farmers to finance the purchase of seeds and fertilisers, Olam always know where their money is going. Chris says this is crucial. It has made it possible for Olam to claim that its products can be traced back to source. Yet Chris seems fairly ambivalent about certification: 'Look, we're certification neutral.' He opens his hands and shrugs his shoulders. 'It's there if our customers want it. And if a customer wants it then we can arrange it.' I can feel a 'but' coming . . . 'But,' he says, 'why do I want someone to tell me that I've done a good job and then charge me for that service and then put their brand on top of our brand?'

Mars has announced that it wants all its cocoa to be sustainably sourced by 2020. Chris says this actually boils down to labelling. 'By this they mean Rainforest Alliance-certified or another certification. Which means in some ways they don't trust us.' For Chris, that's not the solution he would prefer. The really sustainable solution is to be able to make their ethical credentials part of their brand, rather than having to look to certificating bodies to rubber-stamp what they are doing.

Chris clearly believes passionately about what he and his staff, of whom he's fiercely proud, are achieving in Côte d'Ivoire, and he wants them to take the credit they deserve. 'We want Olam to be known as a good company and it dilutes our brand when we have to rely on someone else to certify it.'

Olam have signed up to join the Better Cotton Initiative, an organisation that includes retailers, producers and spinners. Its *raison d'être* is to provide a forum in which better practices can be discussed right through the cotton supply chain. 'They're not there to brand or package. It's more about taking on members who produce cotton in more sustainable ways.' All the big retailers have joined, and so for Olam it's also a good forum to discuss how to make the linkages that they want to make to their farmers. For Chris it's less about PR and ethical certification and more about providing a channel by which to encourage better business.

Concluding thoughts

Outside St Paul's Cathedral, London, a man in a pinstripe suit and red braces walks briskly down Cannon Street in the direction of the City. 'Get a job,' he shouts across the street at the row of a hundred or so tents that have been pitched in front of the church. From behind one of the tents another voice, quick as a flash, shouts back, 'Get a life.'

The St Paul's camp is one of hundreds, known collectively as the Occupy movement, that have sprung up in cities around the world during the second half of 2011. I have come to see if I can get some idea of why it is here.

As I weave my way between the tents, I encounter a man in a pantomime cow suit holding aloft a placard that reads 'PETA [People for the Ethical Treatment of Animals] – Now is the Time to Become a Vegan'. While I am taking it in, he is approached by a young woman whose bag is also emblazoned with the PETA logo. Removing his cow head, the man gratefully takes a cup of warm coffee from her. I can't help noticing that the coffee is in a distinctive Starbucks cup. Behind him is a large banner, hanging between two lamp posts, that asserts 'The Revolution will not be Branded'.

This may appear to be a gross contradiction; and indeed there are other examples of conflicting ideals to be found in the Occupy camp. Instead of one unifying message, all around I can see banners aligned to different causes. Some call on us to use energy more responsibly, others to improve access for estranged fathers or for a review of police brutality. There are young people handing out leaflets that propose an end to capitalism, an end to fossil fuel dependency and even an end to the BBC licence fee.

But despite their seemingly disparate backgrounds and priorities, the Occupy protestors all share an anger and a frustration at how marginalised and voiceless they have become in modern society. Everyone to whom I speak voices a disapproval of how our society has been allowed to develop in the way that it has. Outside one of the larger tents, which serves as the camp's library, I bump into a large set man called Nick. 'I used to be a bailiff,' he tells me. When he read in the papers that eviction notices had been served on the protestors, he decided to come down and lend them his expertise. 'Nobody's going to move these people on until they've been listened to. Nobody,' he assures me with a firm nod of his head.

After two months of protesting without a stated common agenda, things are beginning to stir in the camp and various working groups have formed to focus on specific issues. In the basement of the Caffè Nero across the road, I sit down with the dozen members of Occupy's Economics Working Group. The group have prepared a draft statement that they wish to deliver to the media next week. It outlines what they consider to be the seven most fundamental issues that concern them as 'economists'.

As we sit down to begin the meeting, there's a degree of chit chat. At first, it strikes me as odd that some of the members of the group openly talk about having come to the meeting on the train or from work. Clearly, you don't have to be a camp resident to help find a voice for the cause.

As we work through the individual points, I can hear – in between the angry hyperbole – a list of rather sensible sounding, broad-based ideas coming through. This list includes calls for banks and financial institutions to be more accountable, the economic system to be more sustainable and our society to be more equal. It pleads with the government to regulate more, tax more and take a longer view. While the group is still short of specific policy sugges-tion, they are clear that these kind of sentiments are important if we are to build a fairer society.

The Occupy group are resolutely pragmatic. There's no talk of overthrowing the capitalist system. Capitalism, for all its faults, is still the most effective means we have of lifting people out of poverty. However, there is recognition here that, as we have seen elsewhere, the system is too open to exploitation.

As I listen to the group finalise their statement, I am confident that their focus will eventually reach beyond the banking industry and look at other industries. Banking is but one example of how short-termism, profiteering and unbalanced terms of trade impoverish ordinary people. We have seen how those who grow our food, mine our minerals and assemble our gadgets are exploited by other industries, and how these people, too, demand our attention.

What is needed is development of our current system in a way that protects the most vulnerable and checks the seemingly limitless opportunities that exist for some of the wealthiest members of society to profit at their expense. At its heart, I feel that the Occupy movement is a call for fairness. Fairness in our financial system, yes, but more than that, fairness in the wider global society.

Fairness is about delivering to people what they deserve. The miners of the Congo and the divers of Nicaragua work as hard as anybody for their living. They are not asking for handouts, just a fair slice of the pie that has hitherto been denied to them by an unjust economic system. Fairness should be about reciprocity in exchange – I give you something you want and you give me what I need in exchange. That's not too complex a concept for anyone to grasp.

On the cover of this book I promise to reveal the truth about ethical business. I decided to look for that truth by spending a year living with some of the world's poor, seeing how they work and hearing their stories. I have not sought to provide an exhaustive conclusion, but rather to uncover some individual examples of unfairness perpetrated in the name of big business. Because big business lies at the heart of our system, and one thing I know for sure is that if big business doesn't provide solutions for these people, then there is nothing else I've seen that will.

It tends to be assumed that big business and the interests of workers don't go together. Since the days of inhumane Victorian factories and workshops, big business has been seen more commonly as the cause and not the cure for poverty. But actually it hasn't been this way in every case. Many of the first multi-national businesses demonstrated that business could take its social responsibilities seriously while still making good profits. Cadbury, for instance, heavily influenced by strong Quaker values, provided social housing for workers and eschewed cocoa produced on plantations that used slaves. International conglomerate Unilever was born from the company founded by William Lever, whose enlightened sense of social responsibility led him to build an entire town of decent housing, a town hall and even an art gallery for his employees. Other industrial giants of the time, such as Titus Salt and Edward Akroyd, also invested above and beyond their competitors in better living conditions for workers.

That said, the example set by some of these big companies was rarely followed by others, and over the past 100 years business has generally followed a different route. Forty years ago, the economist Milton Friedman even argued that a business had only one social responsibility: to make as much money as possible for its owners, the shareholders. For Friedman, spending money for general social interest was fine as long it came out of your own pocket. These kinds of investments, he argued, were 'the social responsibilities of individuals not of business'. He claimed one and only one social responsibility for business: 'to use its resources and engage in activities designed to increase its profits'.

In recent times, campaigning groups such as Fairtrade Foundation have been actively seeking to address imbalances in supply chains for coffee, chocolate and the like, but their main achievement has really been to raise awareness rather than to have a truly profound practical impact. Yet the fact that Fairtrade Foundation et al. have been so successful in raising awareness may offer a way forward. Businesses are realising that being socially responsible and making profit are not necessarily mutually exclusive after all. 'Ethical' might not simply now be the 'right' thing to do; it may offer a marketing advantage as well.

Research suggests that the ethical credentials of products are becoming increasingly important to consumers. Big business responds to trends, and the trend at the moment is that 'ethical products' are the fastest-growing sector on the high street. Similarly, the investment landscape on which big business relies is becoming increasingly influenced by ethical factors: over $3 trillion of managed funds in the United States are now following socially responsible investment strategies. What this means is that there may never be a better time to ask how big business is going to engage in more responsible behaviour.

Before you start being responsible, stop being irresponsible

Unfortunately there are still ways in which some companies attempt to 'greenwash' customers by appearing to be more responsible without actually being so. One tactic is to get involved in social projects to demonstrate a commitment to wider social responsibility. Often, though, this is a distraction from the really important issues.

For instance, the crippled young divers who push their wheelchairs through the towns of Nicaragua's coast do not care about reef conservation projects or marine stewardship. The priority for this industry should be to put an end to the atrocious *modus operandi* that regularly results in death and serious injury for the divers, rather than the welfare of the reefs on which they work.

Unfortunately, corporate responsibility does not operate by means of a system of ethical set-offs. It is too easy for big business to see philanthropic donations as a means to an immediate PR win. The logic goes: 'We'll put some money into that charity and then everyone will see how good we are.' But the situation in Nicaragua shows how this is not sufficient.

Philanthropy – thanks, but no thanks

Big businesses sponsor projects and wealthy individuals make donations from vast personal fortunes, but philanthropy alone does not cure poverty. As we saw in China, individual philanthropic causes are by nature unsystematic, often unrelated to need and difficult to predict or guarantee.

Only initiatives that can pay for themselves can be truly long-lasting. Rather than seeking out particular high-profile causes to make donations to, it would be better for companies to embed the desire to improve things in the overall way in which they operate. I saw an example of this in Côte d'Ivoire, when a company whose business was exporting cotton found that they could increase both their own profitability and the local farmers' incomes by providing education and training about cultivation methods. This is a perfect example of core business objectives and social responsibility coming together.

Big business in future will, I believe, need to operate in this way. The reason is part 'carrot' and part 'stick'.

The 'stick': assume that everyone knows everything

First of all, the 'stick'. We live in an age of growing transparency. Campaigning organisations such as Global Witness, WikiLeaks, investigative journalists and people who write books (like this one) are all interested in what big business is up to. Stories about industrial wrongdoing, double standards, pollution, exploitation and corporate greed are stories that sell. What's more, the ability to disseminate these stories is greater than ever. Social media channels like Facebook and Twitter mean that a juicy story about corporate wrongdoing can go global in no time at all.

Big businesses that do operate in a questionable manner, then, are going to be found out. They need to take an inventory check of those issues that could be brand damaging and decide how they are going to resolve them.

The 'carrot': virtue will be rewarded

Of course, many organisations are already engaging in really enlightened initiatives, yet these stories tend to be hidden away on a CSR page on the company website, which no customer is ever going to see. Just as Facebook and Twitter can be used for negative publicity, so too can they be used to shout a business's success from the rooftops. Companies should be thinking now about how to align their responsible business initiatives with their social media strategies.

People like to hear good news, so why not get the best possible PR out of that feel-good factor when you do something positive?

Start at the bottom and work up

Olam, the company investing in cotton farmers in Côte d'Ivoire, offers a superb example of the mutual benefits that can arise from more socially responsible behaviour. The company took control of an area of weakness within their own supply chain, which then enabled them to generate greater efficiencies and therefore higher profits.

Olam also demonstrated that socially responsible initiatives work better if you start at the bottom and work your way up. Local solutions tend to work better than top-down ones. The world's poor are not a homogenous group. Global solutions rarely answer specific needs.

Even once initiatives are established, a long period of hand-holding is often required before they can be sustained independently. As Bente, the benevolent coffee farmer in Tanzania, demonstrated so clearly, the rural poor derive the greatest benefit from having an association with a successful business nearby.

This is the greatest hope for the world's poor. Big business's strengths lie in its ability to manage and innovate. These are the very qualities that are often hardest for the world's poor to engage with. What they need is an injection of know-how and the support to keep using it. Small businesses like the Rare Tea Company and Ethical Addictions, as we saw in Chapter 7, are leading lights in this respect. The challenge is to see how their successes can be applied on a larger scale.

The problem here is currently one of attitude rather than of practicality. Big businesses tend to like big ideas. They often assume that there must be a magic bullet that will solve all deep-rooted issues. The truth is, though, that the obstacles to helping the world's poor are complex and of long standing. There are no global quick-fix solutions. There are, however, lots of local, easy wins that together can make a major contribution. The beauty of operating in this way is that genuine local problems are tackled, lessons are learned and these lessons can then potentially be applied on a larger scale.

The China Factor

Everywhere I went on my travels, I encountered the power of the Chinese economic machine. China may be communist in name, but it is rampantly capitalist in outlook. The jungles of northern Laos provided me with just one of many examples of how China's thirst for natural resources mean that the world's poor are in danger of being overlooked in the name of progress.

Western capitalism struggles against its history of colonialism. As we saw in eastern Congo, we can easily become tied up in ethical conundrums about the rights and wrongs of investing in failing states that blame us for their failure and then end up doing nothing. China acts as though unimpeded by such ghosts. If we're not careful, then, as those Congolese miners who dig in makeshift mines and the middlemen on whom they rely to hawk the minerals they find will testify, our Western ethics naively applied could simply open the door for the less scrupulous to step in. Evolved forms of capitalism, as exist in the West, are a much better solution than the more raw form currently practised in the East.

Outsourcing production doesn't mean outsourcing responsibility

Even within the borders of China, there are worrying signs that some big businesses may not be acting for the benefit for their employees. The country has become the place where low-wage, semi-skilled workers can be found to manufacture, assemble and package goods for Western consumption. It's a tricky situation for the outsourcing company to manage. Am I ethical if the companies to whom I outsource are not ethical?

I think the answer to this question has to be a resounding NO! The products we buy on the high street don't carry the brand of the manufacturing company in China; they carry the brand of the big Western business. As a consumer I have to be able to rely on that brand. How can I make a choice any other way?

This is a good time to tackle the excuse of plausible deniability. It is no longer good enough, in my view, for any big business simply to say that it didn't know something was happening and therefore didn't need to address it. Every big business's responsibility should start with an understanding of the whole supply chain. If something really bad is happening in the production of your product then it's up to you to find it, name it and set about fixing it.

Outsourcing is saving big business countless millions of dollars in production costs, but some of that saving is going to have to be put back into assurance and controls. If companies want to continue to boast of their own ethical credentials, they are going to have to work out how to follow their supply chains all the way back. This is going to require a lot more transparency from big business and also from China. The Internet is already beginning to have a positive effect, as Chinese workers share stories about pay and conditions. It is only a matter of time before that information starts to leak out into the wider world. One has to work on the assumption that what, for example, some Chinese companies now get up to will rebound on the Western companies they supply in due course. We can't claim ignorance any more.

At the heart of this book is a call for more transparency and communication. Customers want reassurance that companies are considering not just how the products they make affect the bottom line but also how they impact on wider society, that all their employees, not just the people in head office but everyone, all the way to the bottom of the supply chain, are treated with dignity and respect and are fairly compensated. The first priority is to ensure that happens; the second is to ensure that customers know about it.

Big business won't do it on its own

The stories I have shared give a snapshot of what life is like for some of the world's poorest people who work hard to supply our needs. The ethically minded consumer who wants to improve the lot of the world's farmers, miners, divers and factory workers has no option but to rely on big business to affect change. Because you can't fly to Tanzania every time you want to buy a cup of coffee or China when you want the latest phone, you must rely on big business as your go-between, your middleman and your link to those people. Our relationship with big business is therefore fundamental if we want things to change but, as with any good relationship, communication is key.

Of course, consumer choice cannot work alone. As I saw in Laos and in Afghanistan, governments need to legislate in such a way as to prohibit the worst practices and encourage the best. But for our part as consumers, we need to keep increasing the proportion of ethical products that fill our shopping baskets. We must also listen to what big business is telling us in return. When a company launches an ethical initiative or a new ethical product, it is up to us to support it, or not. Together we pull the strings of big business through our decision-making, and so we have the power to affect how it operates. Ultimately, we all bear a responsibility.

Index